'*A most fascinating book, and a remarkable piece of rese*[...]
Author of The Outsider (1956), The Occult (1971), M[...]
the Sphinx (1997), Alien Dawn (1998), Dreaming to So[...]

@

'*Intriguing and revelatory, Geoff Ward's Spirals is a stimulating intellectual adventure. There is a great mystery at the heart of existence and the universal symbol of the spiral may be the key.*'   **GRAHAM HANCOCK**
Author of Fingerprints of the Gods (1995/2001), Heaven's Mirror (1999), Keeper of Genesis (with Robert Bauval, 2001), Supernatural (2005)

@

'*I much enjoyed Spirals: the Pattern of Existence. I liked its discursive, antiquarian tone and the lessons Geoff Ward draws from his study of the spiral in nature and ancient traditions.*'   **JOHN MICHELL**
Author of City of Revelation (1972), Ancient Metrology (1981), The New View over Atlantis (1983), New Light on the Ancient Mystery of Glastonbury (1990)

@

'*With impressive research, Geoff Ward reveals the spiral, in one form or another, in an amazing variety of contexts. He invites the reader to see it as a divine unifying clue connecting different realities, from art and ritual to biology and cosmology. The invitation deserves to be taken very seriously.*'   **GEOFFREY ASHE**
Author of King Arthur's Avalon (1957), The Quest for Arthur's Britain (1968), The Ancient Wisdom (1977), Avalonian Quest (1982), The Book of Prophecy (1999)

@

'*During the course of its seven turns, Geoff Ward's engagingly written study, Spirals: the Pattern of Existence, takes us on an exhilarating journey. Impressively comprehensive in its scope, this mind-opening book will provide both intellectual and aesthetic stimulus to the sceptically inclined, and will strengthen the creative intuition of those who trust that there is an underlying order to the complexity of our experience.*' **LINDSAY CLARKE**
Winner of the 1989 Whitbread Prize for Fiction with The Chymical Wedding. Also author of Essential Celtic Mythology (1997, reprinted in 1999 as Lindsay Clarke's Traditional Celtic Stories), The War at Troy (2004) and Return from Troy (2005)

@

'*An absorbing and eloquent book on the meaning of the spiral in human and cosmic terms. The whole range of human knowledge from the earliest times is explored in Geoff Ward's penetrating analysis. The result is a captivating and thought-provoking work which throws new light on the very substratum of the universe. Highly recommended for all lovers of the pulsating curve of life.*'   **PETER MARSHALL**
Author of Nature's Web: rethinking our place on Earth (1996), The Philosopher's Stone: a quest for the secrets of alchemy (2001), World Astrology (2004), Europe's Lost Civilisation: uncovering the mysteries of the megaliths (2004)

@

GEOFF WARD is a journalist, writer and musician who lives in Somerset, England

Spirals
The Pattern of Existence

Geoff Ward

Green Magic

This edition is published by

Green Magic
Long Barn
Sutton Mallet
TA7 9AR
England

Typeset by Academic + Technical, Bristol
Printed and bound by Antony Rowe Ltd, Chippenham

Cover production by Kay Hayden
k.design@virgin.net

ISBN 0 9547 2309 0

GREEN MAGIC

*To Angie, Tyrone, Ramona, James, Sharon
and Paul on their own 'spirals of ascension'*

*Thanks to the following for permission to reproduce the
following illustrations. Nicholas R. Mann, page 5;
Hamish Miller, pages 73 and 74; English Heritage,
page 81; John Martineau, pages 140 and 141;
Alan Richardson, page 150.*

Contents

Introduction

by Colin Wilson

One of the sacred names of the Sphinx of Giza is *neb*, which means 'the spiralling force of the universe'. This seems to indicate that the ancient Eygptians knew about the 'pattern of existence', which is the subject of this remarkable book.

When I was thinking about this introduction, I considered starting with the assertion: 'This book is about the most important subject in the world', then rejected it because it would sound as if I was trying to be provocative. Well, provocative or not, the statement was basically accurate, because the spiral – and the mathematical formula that creates it is virtually a glimpse into the mind of God.

This formula was known to the Greeks as the Golden Section, and was symbolised by the letter φ; it is a way of dividing a painting or piece of architecture into two parts, so that it is oddly pleasing to the eye. Why? I don't know. It is like asking why certain musical phrases give us pleasure. I can only say that when I listen to Mozart's Jupiter Symphony, the introduction of its third subject always gives me a little rush of pleasure, rather like the effect of smelling new-mown hay. It brings about what Proust called a *moment bienheureux*, such as his character Marcel experiences when he tastes a small cake called a madeleine, which he has just dipped in his herb tea. But then, Marcel discovers the reason for this wellspring of delight when he recalls that the taste brings back his childhood in the small town of Combray. But no psychologist has yet discovered why the Golden Section gives us the same kind of pleasure. If I was inclined to be poetic, I might say that it brings back a glimpse of our origin in paradise.

E M Forster touched upon the problem when he remarked that 'War and Peace' produces an 'effect like music'. We know what he means, of course – that the book transports us over great tracts of space and time, and makes us feel oddly detached from the material reality of our everyday lives. But that also fails to explain why a certain phrase of music can produce such an effect.

Let me pause here to get down to some definitions.

When you see bath-water forming into a kind of whirlpool as it goes down the plughole, or observe the pattern of spiral leaf arrangements, or the petals around the edge of a flower, or the shape of a seashell or of a pine cone, or look at a photograph of the Andromeda nebula in a book on astronomy, you are noticing one of the consequences of nature's curious obsession with the spiral, and with the Golden Section.

What is the Golden Section? Well, in its simplest form, it is a way of dividing a line into two parts, one longer than the other, so that the whole line, compared to the longer part, is the same proportion as the longer part compared to the shorter.

The longer part is almost two-thirds of the line – but not quite. Two-thirds would be .666 ... going on forever. The longer part of the Golden Section is .618, but if you go on turning the fraction into a decimal, it also goes on forever without repeating itself.

This number is the basis of the Golden spiral.

The 12th century mathematician Leonardo of Pisa, known as Fibonacci, discovered in 1202 a sequence of numbers that can generate this spiral. Each number in the sequence is made by adding the two previous numbers together. We begin with 0, followed by 1. And since 0 plus 1 make 1, the first Fibonacci number is 1; $1 + 1 = 2$, so the sequence begins 1, 1, 2, then goes on to 3, then 5, then 8, then 13, and so on.

Now represent 1 by a square whose side is 1 unit long, and place it next to another similar square. Now above these place the second square whose sides are 2 units long. And beside these place a square whose sides are 3 units long.

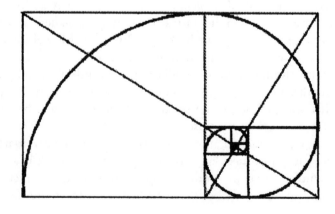

And now if a curved line is drawn that starts in the first square, goes on to touch the far side of the second, then goes up to touch the top of the third square, and so on into the fourth, fifth, etc, the result will be a Fibonacci spiral, which happens to be the spiral you will find in seashells, nebulae, and the rest of the universe.

These Golden proportions can also be found in our bodies, Our navels are placed at .618 of our bodies. If you measure your fingers, you will find that the ratio of the bottom part to the middle, and the middle part to the top joint, is once again the Golden Section proportion.

And why do I find all this so interesting? Because when I began to study these matters, which happened to be in connection with the age of the Sphinx, I quickly became convinced that this piece of knowledge is far, far older than Fibonacci, older than the ancient Greeks, older than the Great Pyramid. The fact that the Sphinx is called by a name that means 'the spiralling force of the universe' seems to suggest that this knowledge predates the ancient Egyptians.

The maverick Egyptologist Schwaller de Lubicz thought that the original ur-civilisation that was the source of this knowledge was Atlantis – which, for various reasons, he believed disappeared at about the time Plato said it did (i.e., around 9500BC). But when I personally took up the quest for the source of ancient knowledge, in a book about the Sphinx, I began to suspect that it could be even older than that.

However, since this Introduction is supposed to be about Geoff Ward and his book, perhaps this is not the place to go into ancient civilisations.

Who is Geoff Ward? I know him as a writer who makes a living by journalism, and who first came to interview me in 2001 to write an article about me. It was excellent and perceptive, and we became friends. Then Geoff started to run a Colin Wilson website, for which I was immensely grateful, since I had always intended to start one of my own, but had always been too busy to get around to it.

When Geoff sent me the typescript of this book, I was amazed to discover that he had embarked on such a complex project. When I wrote to ask him what had led him to launch on such an ambitious design, I received the following reply:

'You may be surprised to learn that it all started with a humble snail! Alfred Watkins' "dodman" to be precise. I had been very interested in megalithic sites, "earth magic" and astro-archaeology since the late Sixties, and in his "The Old Straight Track", Watkins compares the snail with its two horns to the surveyor with his two staves on the ancient trackways, or leys, which Watkins discovered, or perhaps, rediscovered.

'The snail, of course, has a spiral shell and, at the time, I wondered if this had any significance in itself. Then I remembered the spiral tongues of the serpent corbels which I had seen at Kilpeck Church in Herefordshire, not that far from Hereford where Watkins lived (I lived in Herefordshire for a while in the Seventies).

'After I read of dowser Guy Underwood's discovery of spiral energy patterns in the landscape, I started to become aware of the prevalence of spirals in Stone Age art the world over. Like everyone else I was aware of the double helix of the DNA molecule, and then I was struck by the fact that spiral curves were repeated in galaxies in outer space. After that, I was fascinated to find spirals and helices almost everywhere, in both physical and metaphorical manifestations, and was able to make the intuitive leap to guess that the spiral was indeed the 'way' of the universe.

'I suppose I may have been unconsciously seeking a symbol that would at one level connect microcosm and macrocosm, and at another level, science and spirituality. My interests have always been eclectic and this probably helped me to see the connections.

'The next stage was to start seeking out the available literature on the subject, which actually amounted to very few books – those of Cook and Thompson in the early years of the 20th century, and that of Jill Purce in 1974 which seems to have been the first to look at the spiritual aspects of the spiral pattern.

'I rapidly came to see that the spiral was a uniting symbol for all the subjects I was interested in – cosmology, quantum physics, psychology, philosophy, ancient civilisations, megalithic cultures, occult belief systems and even, to a certain extent, literature.

'All this gave me added impetus to investigate further and, as I became aware that there had been no popular study of the subject since Jill Purce (at least in the UK), I thought it would be good idea to produce a new, and wider-ranging, appraisal.'

As can be seen from this letter, Geoff's range of interests is very wide indeed. This I had already gathered from our meeting and correspondence. What surprised me was the range of this present book, and its originality. There is very little with which it can be compared.

Jill Purce, in the opening paragraph of her book, makes it clear that she also sees the Proustian connection: 'In a second, the faintest perfume may send us plummeting to the roots of our being, our whole life verticalised by a fleeting sensation: we have been connected by a mere smell to another place and another time.'

This fascinated me, for I had stumbled upon a very similar concept in the mid-1960s, and subsequently wrote about it in a book called 'The

Occult'. This was the power or ability that I labelled Faculty X, that sudden sense of the reality of other times and other places.

It was an experience of this sort that gave the historian Arnold Toynbee the notion of writing his immense 'Study of History'. It happened in May 1912 as he was musing on the summit of the citadel of Mistra, above the plain of Sparta. Mistra had been a ruin since it had been overrun in the Greek war of independence in the 1820s. Gazing down at the ruins, and nibbling a bar of chocolate, Toynbee was suddenly carried back to that day when the invaders had poured into Mistra and massacred most of the inhabitants; from that day onward it had remained a ruin. Suddenly, time stood still and the past became a living reality.

Toynbee experiencd several such 'time slips', which he describes in a passage in the tenth volume. One concerned a Cretan villa of one of the last of the Venetian governors. As he stood looking at this deserted house he 'had an experience which was the counterpart, on the psychic plane, of an aeroplane's sudden deep drop when it falls into an air-pocket'. He was 'carried down a time-pocket' to a day two hundred and fifty years ago when the house was suddenly evacuated and deserted.

This image of the aeroplane dropping into an air pocket bears an obvious resemblance to Jill Purce's image. But she obviously feels that what has happened in that Proustian glimpse is a sudden connection to a lower level of the spiral of our own existence.

I say all this to underline that what we are speaking of here is not some abstract arithmetical concept. It is directly connected to one of the most important secrets of human existence. It is that sudden moment of contact with the sense of power and purpose inside us.

What is so interesting is that this nerve is also touched when we are in contact with ancient sites that are connected with this 'spiral energy'. Geoff explains in his fourth chapter, 'Dragon Magic' how 'even as a small child I was attracted to, and moved by both sites of antiquity . . . and the patterns the stars made in the sky'. And he goes on to speak of Maiden Castle, and how 'the old stones stand . . . as a reminder . . . of something important the human race has lost, or at least forgotten'.

I stumbled on the same discovery in the mid-1970s when I came upon the work of T C Lethbridge, to whom I dedicated a large part of my book 'Mysteries'. Lethbridge, a Cambridge archaeologist, was also a highly gifted dowser; and when he left Cambridge (sick of the triviality and backbiting of his fellow dons) in 1957, and moved to an old house at Branscombe in Devon, he embarked on the most interesting stage of his career, as he began to discover the extraordinary power of the long pendulum, and its ability to read the secrets of landscape. He became convinced that the dowser's pendulum can respond to other levels of reality that somehow co-exist with this one. In recent years, these discoveries have been taken up by the rock musician Julian Cope, and by my friend Terry Welbourn, who has formed a group of like-minded landscape archaeologists who call themselves 'the Sons of T C Lethbridge'.

It seems to me that Geoff Ward has stumbled upon this same subject by a kind of inspiration, and that he has written a book that will become a classic of forgotten knowledge. He seems to have the field virtually to himself. I am delighted to play my small part in launching his voyage of intellectual discovery upon the world.

1

Into the Swirl

'In the fury of the moment I can see the Master's hand,
In every leaf that trembles, in every grain of sand.'

Bob Dylan (1941–), *Every Grain of Sand,* 1981

The spiral is the sign of the eternal, creative, unifying and organising force or principle at work in the universe, and especially of the ongoing creation of consciousness. It is a divine mark on nature, what may be termed God's personal signature on the cosmos, the Great Architect's own autograph – from the cradles of stars and planets in the awesome spiral arms of galaxies to the beautiful double helix structure of the DNA molecule, from the 'dragon currents' of earth energies to the vortices of whirlpools and weather systems, from the volutes of sea waves to the hair on our heads which grows in a spiral about the crown.

As the spiral seems to be integral to physical growth, so it is also the symbolic pattern of human spiritual growth. Ancient man took the cosmic cue and made talismanic magic from it to help to keep his society in harmony with the universe, rather than at odds with it as so many of our activities are today.

The significance of this signature, which wondrously reveals the *karma* of the universe in visible action, has been largely forgotten or ignored, or at best taken for granted nowadays. Yet it remains within us as the image of all creation, and still moves purposefully and behind events which influence our existence on this planet. But its power as a symbol infused with magical and mystical meaning is being reawakened for, existentially, the spiral is as much part of our 'cultural DNA' as it is part of our biological DNA.

Indeed, I have come to realise that 'spirality' – the condition of being spiral – and 'reality' are almost interchangeable terms.

1

We can all visualise a spiral, and visualisation is the first step towards magic. One key to an explanation of the pre-eminence of the pattern lies in the idea common to both the Kabbalah, in which the Serpent of Wisdom is depicted coiling itself in a spiral about the Tree of Life, and to occultists and magicians over the ages, that all things in the universe are part of an organised whole. This idea is summed up in the dictum 'as above, so below', attributed to Hermes Trismegistus ('three times great'), the Greek name given to the Ancient Egyptian god of wisdom Thoth, who was the patron of alchemists, the legendary founder of magic, and believed to be the scribe of the gods and the inventor of writing and all arts dependent upon it, including astronomy, magic and medicine, as well as a guide to the souls of the dead. The Hermetic tradition embraced a Gnostic heresy which repudiated the necessity for, or existence of, a supreme being, and regarded the individual as potentially a demigod whose mind was capable of encompassing universal knowledge and who could aspire to divine status. Thus the Elizabethan playwright and poet Christopher Marlowe (1564–93), who would have been familiar with the 'Corpus Hermeticum', was able to write in 'Dr Faustus' that 'a sound magician is a mighty god'. In a sense, our Hermetic heritage occupies an important position looking back to Gnosticism and forward to a positive existentialism which would be concerned to see the beneficial fulfilment of human evolutionary potential.

We shall indeed discover, in the course of this book, the significance of the spiral form above and below, at all levels from the cosmological to the sub-atomic, and that the spiral way is indeed the way of the universe. As no lesser personage than John D Barrow, Professor of Mathematical Sciences and Director of the Millennium Mathematics Project at Cambridge University, has said, we need to appreciate more fully how the cosmic environment imprints itself on our minds and bodies in ways that shape their structures, fascinations and biases.

In 'The Artful Universe Expanded' (2005), Barrow, whose researches in cosmology have been indicative of the way in which more enlightened sectors of contemporary science are catching up on the ancients' intuitive understanding of the cosmos, says: 'The propensities and sensitivities of the human mind have been inherited from the complexity of the environment in which it has evolved and acclimatised. We reflect many of the features of the laws of nature and the structure of the universe around us.' As above, so below, indeed.

The authors of the Hermetic writings are unknown and it is likely that they spanned several centuries, the earliest being the second or third century BC. One of the underlying Hermetic beliefs was that the universe or cosmos was a unity and that all of its parts were interdependent, but that the laws which governed the relationship between these parts could be understood only by divine revelation. The ancient wisdom regarded the whole universe as being alive, in great contrast to the modern scientific approach which has taken the opposite view, that it incorporates 'dead' matter.

The Greeks and Romans involved themselves deeply in mysticism, astrology and magic, incorporating them into their belief systems and theurgical outlook with the aim of intensifying a person's personal experience of the numinous and his or her understanding of the universe. The Hermetic system of occult sympathies, or correspondences, which also underlies much of the tradition of natural magic, aims to reveal secret but beneficial links between apparently unconnected aspects of the universe. These beneficent forces do not operate upward from below, but downwards from above.

That such links exist, in terms of physical energy, is in little doubt today, but ancient astrologers often made conscious attempts to emulate heavenly events by constructing or identifying sacred places in accordance with the movements of the stars and planets, or by celebrating festivals when a certain star or planet was on the ascendant.

The Tree of Life, indeed, is fundamental to the Kabbalah (from the Hebrew 'to receive'), which is a system of Jewish gnostic religious philosophy, practised from about the seventh century onwards, and arriving in western Europe during the Renaissance period. The Tree of Life is interpreted both as a view of the different levels of the macrocosm of the universe, how it develops in a series of stages from a night of Brahma into full embodiment, and as a microcosm embracing human spiritual development, and involves especially the various initiatory paths that must be pursued if enlightenment and finally, complete gnosis, is to be achieved.

It also acts as an illustration of how God diffused himself into the void in order to create the universe, which came into being because God wanted to know himself and also express his love through that creative act, and then experience what he had created by manifesting himself in the worlds he had brought into existence. All aspects of Creation arise from the unfolding of God's Will, which reveals itself through a series of ten emanations represented on the Tree of Life – the lowest earth and the highest, God – which are known as the sephirah (sephiroth, singular), connected by 22 paths, each represented by one of the 22 letters of the Hebrew alphabet. These paths are used by the Kabbalist to ascend to a state of reintegration with God, and their representation is a veritable 'blueprint' of the universe, and of life and consciousness within it.

In humans, the ten emanations can be represented by levels of consciousness, and according to magical philosophy, the most effective way of changing the world is to change your own consciousness, to move up to a higher plane. The central work of Kabbalistic lore is 'The Zohar', largely a commentary on the Pentateuch, the first five books of the Old Testament, but also explaining how an initiate can win control of the supernatural world of spirits.

In mysticism, 'as above, so below' indicates that the human soul and God are one and the same. In magic, man is the microcosm, his symbol being the five-pointed star, or pentacle, and the universe at large is the macrocosm, with its symbol being the six-pointed star, as in the Great Seal of Solomon with which Solomon controlled the legions of demons, a power associated with him not only in Jewish magical traditions, but in Arabic and Greek too.

The six-pointed star is formed out of two interconnecting triangles which represent the masculine and feminine principles. Within them, standing for the dualities of essence and substance, a descending spiral represents the creation of matter from spirit – an idea which seems to have presaged today's concept of radiant energy in space transforming itself into matter – and an ascending spiral man's return path.

Solomon and Moses represented the Jewish thread of such magical traditions, as Thoth had represented the Ancient Egyptian, and Hermes Trismegistus, the Graeco–Roman. We will see how, within such traditions over the centuries, the spiral gained talismanic properties through being charged with spiritual, emotional and/or intellectual energy.

Occultists believed that all things were governed by secret laws, with hidden connections or correspondences between many things which on the surface did not appear to be linked; connections which are becoming familiar to us today as theories in high energy physics, astrophysics and molecular and evolutionary biology converge in an attempt to answer the ultimate question of how the universe and life came into being.

Connections as we talk of the 'life spiral' or the 'evolutionary spiral', even the 'inflationary spiral', and as we frequently read in news reports of the 'downward spiral' to dissipation or the spiralling upwards of costs or some other quantitative feature – such figurative expressions being used without general recognition of their metaphysical derivations. The words 'evolution', 'devolution', 'revolution', all arise from the Latin root *volute* which indicates a spiral or scroll-shaped form or movement.

4

The occultists' notion was that all phenomena contained something of the divine and that man, on a tiny scale, was a reflection of God and of the universe. The idea of a path that could be climbed in stages to reach God was fundamental to both the Kabbalah and exponents of magic down the centuries, the archetypal image of the spiral coming to render itself in the three- and two-dimensional initiatory mazes which existed in antiquity.

It is believed that such three-dimensional mazes, or processional pathways, existed, for example, at Glastonbury Tor in Somerset, Godshill on the Isle of Wight, and at Silbury Hill in Wiltshire. The one at the Tor may have been constructed as long as 5,000 years ago, according to certain estimates. Pilgrims would have entered such a maze part way

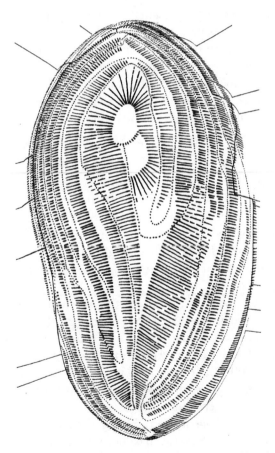

The Glastonbury Tor spiral maze – perhaps 5,000 years old. The Tor is symbolic of the World Mountain or Omphalos.

up the side of the hill and travelled first in a clockwise, then in an anti-clockwise, direction making their way to the holy summit, possibly by means of seven full circuits, absorbing the energy of the natural 'power station' as they went.

The theory of a spiral maze at the Tor, put forward by Geoffrey Russell in the 1960s was confirmed by the Arthurian scholar Geoffrey Ashe in the following decade. More recently, the Glastonbury historian Nicholas Mann has said that the Tor, whether or not its terraces were carved in pre-history, is the 'prototypical sacred and spiral mountain', and, along with Silbury Hill, represents the symbolic World Mountain of old, the *omphalos*, where above and below, the sky opening and the underworld, conjoin. The idea of a world-centre has long been associated with the spiral motif.

'The inward spiral represents an inner voyage of discovery. One follows this path to discover the inner realities of one's own existence to the centre, and having found the centre one starts on the outer spiral path of development, bringing with you those inner discoveries, and from which you emerge transformed. One may well find that one enters and walks out of the spiral several times in one's life.'

Kevin Saunders, *Wiccan Spirituality*, 2001

Ancient mazes and labyrinths, often symbolising the unconscious with its unknown capabilities and potentialities, indicated a relationship between a 'charged' centre and a difficult or circuitous access, and their provenance was infused with a magical or numinous quality.

They occur worldwide and throughout history, in varying forms and are made out of varying materials, largely based on the 'classical' design of a series of concentric lines, at the core of which is the figure that creates the *ankh*, used by the Ancient Egyptians to secure the restoration of the living spirit. Thus the labyrinth appears on Egyptian seals and was the basis of the design of a number of pharaohs' tombs which had convoluted access corridors and false entries. One such classical design, dated to 1800BC, can be found in two carvings close together on a rock face in Rocky Valley, near Tintagel in Cornwall.

It is possible to envisage the classical labyrinth pattern having evolved from observation of the radiating formations in seed heads and pine cones for, as Jeff Saward has pointed out, this would involve merely tracing a spiral through the points that comprise the seed, or over-laying the seed with a spiral.

One of the two labyrinth carvings at Rocky Valley, near Tintagel, Cornwall, dated to 1800BC.

Alternatively, labyrinths may have been derived from ritual dances which described a kind of spiral, not one turning in towards a centre, but one that turned back on itself, moving both clockwise and anti-clockwise, and in and out, until a centre was finally reached, and then moving back out to the perimeter.

Indeed, there were ritual 'labyrinth' dances of old, with steps spiralling symbolically in and out, perhaps originally in imitation of serpent gods. Theseus, returning from Crete after killing the Minotaur, and stopping at the island of Delos to sacrifice in thanksgiving to Apollo, danced with his companions the Crane Dance, or the Geranos, the intricate patterns of which imitated the winding passages of the labyrinth. This dance, so named for its erratic, high-stepping moves, was still being performed on Delos well into the historical period, and has been revived in that region in recent times.

For thousands of years, the ritual dance has been a means of opening up the unconscious mind and generating positive psychic energy, possibly developing from the movements of early tribal shamans. Indeed, one of these dances has become known as the 'spiral dance', an embellishment of the simple circle dance in which people join hands and skip or run around the circumference of a sacred circle or fire.

A clockwise direction for the dancers is referred to as deosil, following the direction of the sun's movement across the sky, and is the opposite of widdershins, the left-handed or 'sinister' movement. The circular motion is modified to move inwards towards the centre of the circle and then out again, tracing a spiral pattern, and symbolising an entry into the mysteries of the 'Otherworlds'.

In Wicca, the nature-based religion which has the Great Goddess as its principal deity, this is known specifically as the spiral dance, and this was the title of the first book by Starhawk (Miriam Simos), one of the foremost promoters of the new Goddess-based spirituality. The book was first published in 1979, becoming a best-seller in American neo-pagan and witchcraft circles and a classic in the Wiccan canon.

In it, Starhawk refers to the shamans who guided hunting tribes tens of thousands of years ago, and who could 'attune themselves to the spirits of the herds, and in so doing they became aware of the pulsating rhythm that infuses all life, the dance of the double spiral, of whirling into being, and whirling out again . . . The spiral dance was seen also in the sky: in the moon who monthly dies and is reborn; in the sun, whose waxing light brings summer's warmth and whose waning brings the chill of winter'.

Michael Jordan, in his 'Ceremonies for Life', refers to a traditional meeting dance in Somerset, England, a special form of the spiral dance used by pagans at the start of a ritual: 'Everyone joins hands in the circle, men and women alternating. Each faces outwards and begins to dance anti-clockwise, or widdershins, in the direction of death . . . The priestess suddenly releases her left hand and leads the dance inwards in a gradual spiral until the dancers have come together in the centre of the circle. She turns to her right and kisses the man next to her in a symbolic awakening to new life before leading the dancers in an expanding clockwise, or deosil, spiral following the sun and the rebirth of life. Each woman likewise kisses a man as she passes him.'

'The many musets through the which he goes
Are like a labyrinth to amaze his foes.'

William Shakespeare (1564–1616), *Venus and Adonis,* 1593

8

Appearing in Minoan Crete, a labyrinth designed by Daedalus was part of the Minotaur legend and the bull cult which it embodied, and the labyrinth motif was received in Greece by 1500BC. In Greek mythology, Ariadne tells Theseus that the labyrinth is made up of a left-handed, septenary spiral path coiling in, and a right-handed path coiling out.

Built about 1900BC, the first major palace at Knossos, Crete, was probably known as the Labyrinth, and Troy, after the siege dated to about 1250–1220BC, was symbolised by the labyrinth, and many later labyrinths made of rocks in Scandinavia, and of turf in Britain and Germany, became known as 'Troy Towns' in tribute to the archetypal city and its daunting defences. Jerusalem, too, and Jericho, became associated with the labyrinth and a number of pavement labyrinths in French cathedrals were called *chemin de Jerusalem*, or 'Road to Jerusalem'.

The Walls of Troy, Rockliffe Marsh, Cumbria

In India, the labyrinth represented both a protective symbol and the layout of the defences of cities and military formations. In particular, the defences of the city of Scimangada, in the foothills of the Himalayas in Nepal, and now lying in ruins, were depicted as a symbol of the labyrinth.

The idea of the labyrinth-tomb became widespread and survived into later ages, being taken up by the Celts, for example. Roman mosaic labyrinths were discovered at Cirencester, Gloucestershire, and reburied for protection. In Britain and Ireland, the maze spiral, in both left- and right-handed forms, appears carved on the walls of prehistoric burial chambers, and mazes were also cut in the turf near ancient earthworks in villages and on hillsides, such as at Julian's Bower, Alkborough, Lincolnshire, and the Mizmazes at St Catherine's Hill, overlooking

Winchester, near Breamore, Hampshire, and also at Leigh in Dorset (this one ruinous and overgrown). Altogether, forty turf mazes are known in Britain; many date from the Middle Ages but some are much older.

A medieval labyrinth in ornate form as inlaid in the floor of Chartres Cathedral, about 1205.

The maze was adopted by Christianity to signify the difficulty of reaching Heaven, and in the Middle Ages some churches had mazes drawn on their floors along which, it is alleged, penitents prostrated themselves towards a centre known as the 'Heavenly Jerusalem'. The most famous of the medieval Christian labyrinths is the splendidly preserved 13th century pavement labyrinth in Chartres Cathedral, an ideal example of the circumambulatory movement, now nearer, now further away, from the centre along twisting paths which absorb all the surrounding space. Hereford's famous late 13th century Mappa Mundi represents Crete with a labyrinth design, and at St Mary Redcliffe Church, Bristol, there is a unique decorative gilded roof boss, dating from the 1390s, in the shape of a medieval labyrinth.

'The design of many labyrinths reproduces, in the main, the cosmic city layout in tangible form, a plan microcosmically related to the archetypal city (Jerusalem or Troy), which was itself a microcosm of the first concept of the world, whose centre was traditionally Jerusalem.'

Nigel Pennick (1946–), founder of the Institute of Geomantic Research, *The Ancient Science of Geomancy*, 1979

Across the globe, at Casa Grande in the southern Arizona desert, a classical labyrinth pattern is etched on the wall of the Hohokam tower house which was built in the 14th century, although the labyrinth drawing is believed to have been added later, possibly by a member of the Piman people who are known to have used the symbol.

Hundreds of garden mazes and labyrinths planted in Britain from the 17th to the 19th centuries have long since disappeared, as trends in garden design have come and gone, but a number have survived, including one at Glendurgan House in Cornwall, planted in 1833, a yew hedge maze at Madresfield Court, Herefordshire, dating from the late 19th century, and another at Brockenhurst, Hampshire, where the famous Hampton Court maze was copied in about 1890.

The labyrinth was joined inseparably with the mystery of life and death. Its false tracks and cul-de-sacs symbolised the sins and temptations which men and women had to resist on the journey to Heaven. As the mandala, or 'chart' of the progression of the soul, the symbolic spiritual journey along the spiral, towards God without or God within, depending on the direction travelled, through pilgrimage or meditation, appears in numerous traditions and cultures, representing the fusion and flow of dynamic opposites balanced in universal harmony, as exemplified in the Chinese yin-yang symbol.

The beauty of the labyrinth design is not just aesthetic, or to do with its universal appeal, but also in the fact that, as it is not claimed by any one faith or tradition, the individual can draw from its pathways whatever he or she desires, and use it as an aid to healing and meditation. Many people today design and build their own labyrinths with this purpose in mind, on beaches and in gardens or in other open spaces, using a range of materials, stone or wood, for example, or simply a design chalked on a concrete or tarmac surface.

The three circles, or planes, of spiritual evolution found in Druidic philosophy seem also to imply a spiral progression: the plane of Annwn, the great cauldron or creative void, gives rise to the material or human world of Abred which, in turns, leads to Gwynvyd, the plane of the fully developed spirit. On the first plane, matter is created, on the second, it takes physical form, and on the third, it attains perfection. It was the Cauldron of Annwn which, by way of Celtic myth, may have formulated the symbol of the Holy Grail, the legend of which, while cultivated for Christian purposes, may well be derived entirely from Druidical sources, and which has links to the classical Greek myth of the 'horn of plenty', or *cornucopia*, the horn of the goat Amalthea which suckled the infant Zeus, and which frequently appears in a spiral shape.

11

The Grail Castle, indeed, could be the palace of Caer Sidi, which has been rendered in English as 'spiral castle', in Annwn. Caer Sidi is mentioned in a poem, 'The Spoils of Annwn', credited to the sixth-century Welsh bard Taliesin who, in some representations, is actually depicted as being born from a spiral form. Also translated as 'Circle of Revolution', Caer Sidi was the temple of the Ceridwen, the Earth Mother (and Taliesin's mother) and goddess of nature. Arianrhod, the Welsh goddess of time, *karma* and reincarnation, was said to dwell in a citadel at the centre of a spiral path.

The Welsh bards knew the Druids as *naddred*, or adders, which was probably an allusion to the Druids' supposed 'rebirth' as initiates into the order, making an allegorical reference to the serpent which sheds its skin. The legend is that Druid leaders were descended from one Bran who 'in the sultry plains of Asia' – hinting at the region from which it is believed the Druidic movement originated – seized the sacred serpent's egg which, conferring wisdom, power and dignity, became the cult's talisman, the arch-druid wearing it on a golden chain about his neck. Druidism is really only the Egyptian cult of Osiris in another guise, both Osiris and Britain's King Arthur originating in a common source of myth of the hero who must die but is to be reborn.

In Europe and the Middle East, the seven-fold spiral (a spiral taking seven turns about its centre) has had special connections with the origin of the universe and of life. The seven turns symbolised and re-enacted the primeval creative process. The seven-fold spiral is also to be found among the Hopi indians of the American South-West who regard it as a Mother Earth symbol. The earliest spiral known in the history of art, the ur-heptad, relating the magical number of seven to a centre, is drawn on a mammoth ivory found by archaeologists at Mal'ta in Siberia. It is about 23,000 years old and linked with the lost civilisation of Shambhala, possibly the legendary land of the Hyperboreans, said to lie in the Altai Mountains.

It is here, more than 5,000 years ago, that the seven-stage spiral labyrinth may have been invented, then taken west to Britain with the Celts and Druids in later times, and spreading south also to other parts of Europe and the Middle East. The Druids seem to have recognised the source of the seven mystique as the seven stars of the constellation Ursa Major, although in Britain they knew the pattern as the 'seven stars of Arthur'.

The great *ziggurat* of Babylon, the original Tower of Babel, was called the Etemenanki, the 'Temple of the Foundation of Heaven and Earth', and its holy summit was reached by a spiral path ascending through seven tiers. Similarly, the final phase of the construction of the

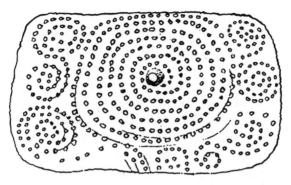

The oldest spiral known in the history of art – drawn with seven turns on a mammoth ivory in Siberia, and dating from about 23,000 years ago.

4,500-year-old Silbury Hill comprised six terraces of chalk, with the seventh level being the summit. The septenary spiral has been interpreted as the 'world centre' motif employed by Shambhala to convey its once dominant position as a seat of wisdom and knowledge.

Shambhala evidently had high regard for the seven stars of the constellation Ursa Major which, according to the poet and mystic Gerald Massey (1828–1907) in *The Natural Genesis*, 1883, were probably 'the primordial figure of seven'. Certainly, the constellation would have been prominent in the night skies above the northern latitudes of the Altai Mountains. Massey made a connection between the constellation and the septenary spiral labyrinth, the number of volutions of which about the centre represented 'the seven encirclers of the Great Bear'. Bears have been powerful magic in religion throughout history and have been said to be the oldest of verifiable divine beings, being revered even by Neanderthal man more than 50,000 years ago, and later associated with Artemis and the Sun god Apollo, whose origins lay with the Hyperboreans. It came to be popularly believed that the bear was born an amorphous mass but that when 'licked into shape' he symbolised an ordered universe fashioned out of original chaos.

A link between the number seven and wisdom is to be found in the Bible where Wisdom personified (Sophia) implies that she helped God to bring order out of primal chaos (in six days and resting on the seventh), or perhaps in the parlance of modern day astrophysicists, from the outspilling of matter from the original black hole or 'cosmic gusher' which led to the formation of the universe. In chapter eight of Proverbs, Wisdom says: 'The Lord possessed me in the beginning of his way, before his works of old. I was set up from everlasting, from the beginning, or even the earth was.'

Seven, of course, is a number that has had special resonance throughout human history: the colours of the rainbow, the notes of the Western musical scale, the seven deadly sins, the seven days of the week, and so on. It is also the number of levels of consciousness in the Kabbalah, and of planetary spheres in ancient astrology, and by way of recognition of this magical number, both explanatory and symbolic, I have divided this book into seven chapters.

Desmond Varley, in his study of the significance attached to the number seven, described the spiral as the symbol of the evolutionary process, and a representation of the cycles of time. 'When no further evolution is possible, the spiral becomes a simple circle, the sign of eternity or that which is outside time,' he adds. Certainly, the spiral has a special relationship with the number seven, for both are creation symbols. Varley suggests the special significance of the number seven stems from a distant time of global catastrophe when three heavenly bodies, or 'gods', the Sun, Moon and a minor planet, the latter crashing into the Earth, stirred up the four elements, earth, air, fire and water.

Seven: the number of creation, 1976

Michael Hayes, in *High Priests, Quantum Genes*, 2004, shows that the number seven, along with three and 22, occur repeatedly in the world's major religions. The number *pi*, which is the relation of a diameter of a circle to its circumference, is 22 divided by seven, and is the cornerstone of what Hayes calls the Hermetic Code, after Hermes Trismegistus, the Greek version of Thoth, the ancient Egyptian god of wisdom and writing. Hayes argues convincingly that the ordering principles of the universe, the fundamental processes of life and evolution, are embodied in an age-old numerical pattern reflected in the structure of music. Certainly, our seven–note musical scale can be represented easily as a spiral progression, each eighth note, or octave, standing at a higher or lower turn of a spiral.

14

The Biblical Garden of Eden envisaged a Tree of Knowledge of Good and Evil which was guarded by a serpent often depicted, as in Michelangelos's ceiling of the Sistine Chapel, with its coils spiralling tightly around the trunk. It was this reptile that offered the forbidden fruit of the knowledge of good and evil – in effect, the ability to make moral and abstract judgements – to Adam and Eve. For this, as recounted in the third chapter of Genesis, God cursed the serpent, saying 'upon thy belly thou shalt go', resulting in the Church's subsequent erroneous identification of the serpent or dragon with evil, instead of with its usual beneficent links with fertility, life-enhancement, vital energy and harmony with the universe. Indeed, the Ancient Egyptians made the serpent their emblem of intellectual power, and in the later Gnostic tradition it came to represent wisdom.

At Prayag, modern-day Allahbad, at the confluence of the Ganges and Jumna rivers, in northern India – a holy place which is the scene of a great annual religious festival – there is a shrine to a primeval serpent which guards an eternal tree; it is the only shrine of its kind in India. Prayag was regarded as being the navel of the Earth, the location of a World Mountain rising out of life-giving waters, and the place where heaven and earth first separated. Ancient Eridu, the site of the first shrine of Sumer, 'the cradle of civilisation', also honoured a sacred tree and a mound of creation, and was perhaps the inspiration for the Garden of Eden. Again, we are encountering a universal myth, also found, for example, at Teotihuacan, Mexico, Cuzco, Peru, and Hierakonpolis in Upper Egypt, not to mention Glastonbury in England, clear evidence that the human mind favours certain symbols, and has the same dream of a bridge from earth and heaven, even though societies may be oceans and thousands of years apart.

It has been speculated that, bearing in mind the worldwide pervasiveness of dragon myths, the Biblical story of the Fall relates allegorically to an evolution of human intelligence caused by the fear which dinosaurs inspired in the precursors of mankind, the biological recollection of which still resides in the collective unconscious. The terror which predators instilled may later have contributed to the belief in dragons, demons and gods of the underworld.

Serpent cults have persisted the world over since prehistoric times, with a spiral corresponding to the coiled or resting posture of the creature, and a zigzag for its sinuous movement, and have been the enactors of much accompanying ritual, including those dances with serpentine movements. The powerful imagery in such ancient rituals extended deep into the collective, or communal, imagination, and mythologies worldwide are infused with it. Ancient communities, and those with long-surviving traditions, understood the importance of such rituals, and gave close attention to their complete and graphic enactment. The serpent was believed to control fertility, was always associated with water and the advent of new life and creative energy, and frequently with the Moon; no other animal has given rise to a more potent or pervasive tradition.

It is my belief that serpent cults were the result of an intuitive understanding of the significance and prevalence of the spiral form in nature; that the coils of the snake, effectively, were superimposed on the spiral pattern and became a homomorphic representation of its qualities and potentials in the immediate world.

Philip Gardiner and Gary Osborn, in their interesting book 'The Serpent Grail' (2005), claim that the Holy Grail, the Elixir of Life and the Philosopher's Stone are all metaphors for spiritual enlightenment which can be traced back directly to the ancient worship of the snake – as representative of the primary force behind creation – for its life-giving properties, and to its relationship to shamanic ritual. The cover of their book shows a snake with its coils spiralling around a golden chalice. However, the authors regard the spiral as the symbol of the snake when actually it is the other way round – the snake, as depicted in ritual art and so on, is a symbol of the spiral. Gardiner and Osborn thus are unable to make the crucial link between serpent cults and the spiral, although it is clear that their perceptive contention that religious movements grew out of serpent-worship is strengthened, if not validated, by the spiral connection.

The spiral progression – re-volution or re-evolution – is symbolic of the transpersonal route to that higher level of consciousness which is sought by all esoteric and occult systems. Such movements in physical space parallel those inner movements of the psyche which indicate the transformative and the integrative; there is also the circumambulatory, as utilised in mazes and labyrinths; oscillation, the movement back and forth between dualities; and the vortex, or involution, representing an opening or re-awakening.

As physicist John Hitchcock recognised, the circumambulatory and oscillative suggest the mandala, the symbol of wholeness, while the spiral and the vortex point to dynamic growth and metamorphosis. Indeed, we shall see how the spiral vortex, as found in the movement of water and in the structure of the DNA molecule, in just two examples, is nature's favoured form for the transmission of its energy, both economically and efficaciously, radiating out and drawing in simultaneously; infinitely and eternally.

In Carlos Castenada's 'Tales of Power', don Juan, the old Yaqui indian *brujo*, conjures up a fellow sorcerer from moving spirals of ashes released from under a hat, and later, in 'The Second Ring of Power', Castenada is told how a spiralling gust of wind enveloped dona Soledad and gave don Juan the means of achieving her 'transformation'. Moreover, in 'The Eagle's Gift', don Juan is reported as saying that losing the human form – the only means of liberating one's 'core of awareness' and arriving at the totality of oneself – is like a spiral allowing freedom to remember the self, and in turn making one feel even more free.

Some thinkers, like the eminent Swiss psychologist Carl Gustav Jung, whose work we shall be looking at in the next chapter, stress the universal nature of this higher consciousness, which complements the idea that at transcendent levels of awareness the self becomes superfluous and the soul becomes one with its cosmic origins.

'Old secrets rise to the surface and dissolve into the consciousness of the human race to fertilise the seed of evolutionary growth. The important discoveries about the past have been made not so much through the present refined techniques of treasure hunting and grave robbery, but through the intuition of those whose faith in poetry led them to a scientific truth. The gradual accumulation within each succeeding generation of the total knowledge of the past through the hereditary medium, known to biologists as DNA, is a phenomenon of which we have again become conscious, and this realisation ensures the ultimate re-establishment of the former belief in revelation on which the science of the ancient world was founded.'

John Michell (1933–), *The View Over Atlantis*, 1969

WHORLS OF WORDS

Etymologically, the word 'spiral' springs from ancient roots inextricably bound up with ideas of creation, life-giving and aspiration – from the Latin *spiralis* or *spira*, and the Greek *speira*, meaning a spire or coil, or a conical or pyramidal structure, as well as from the Latin *spirare*, meaning 'to breathe,' as in expire and inspire. The definition of 'spire', in addition to being a tall, slender architectural structure tapering to a point, is to put forth shoots or sprouts, obviously signifying birth and rebirth.

Tellingly, our word 'spirit', representing the animating, non-material divine element in humans which gives life and reason, is drawn from the same semantic origins. Spirit, of course, is the vital, fundamental principle of existence, as well as those personal qualities such as courage, pride and vivacity of mind. It is interesting that the most spiritual animal, in the classical view, is the snake. And when you read the word 'spiritual', have you ever noticed that you are seeing 'S-P-I-R-(itu)-A-L'?

A spiracle is a respiratory orifice, such as the whale's blowhole which, as will be suggested in a later chapter, is a term which can also be used in connection with the origin of the universe and the continuing creation of matter within it.

'Helix' is Greek for spiral, and relates to the Greek *helissein*, meaning 'to turn round', although in mathematics a spiral is accepted as a curve on a plane which winds around a fixed point – as in the spiral of information on a compact disc which, typically, is three miles long! – and a helix as a curve on a developable surface, as exemplified on a cylinder, in the thread of nuts and bolts, or in the rifling of a gun barrel; such a curve would turn into a straight line if the surface was unrolled.

Helix, or helice, is also the name for the willow tree, the branches of which, like those of the hazel, are used to make the divining rods with which dowsers can detect currents of earth energy, underground streams or buried objects. In electricity, a spiral coil of wire wound round a bobbin can be utilised as an armature to concentrate a current, which calls to mind the spirally patterned concentrations of energy traced by dowsers and geomancers, not only in the landscape but also around people, plants and trees.

A helicon is a bass or contrabass tuba, built in a spiral form, which rests on the shoulder. It is believed to have been invented in Russia but was perfected in 1849 by Ignaz Stowasser in Vienna.

The word 'spicule' comes from the Latin *spica*, meaning an ear of corn. Spica is the name of the first magnitude star in the constellation of Virgo, and it is also a word which means a spiral bandage with reversed turns, suggesting an ear of barley. Virgo, the Virgin, is represented by a serpent, as are certain other of the zodiacal signs. Serpents and ears of corn are both trappings of Druidism, as well as of Mithraism. A spicula is a snail's dart. Spiraster, incorporating the Greek word *aster*, meaning 'star', is a coiled sponge-spicule with radiating spines.

Mercury, or Hermes, the deity of leys, rules Virgo whose coiling serpent symbol is found as part of Hermes' staff, or heraldic wand, the caduceus, usually depicted with two intertwined serpents in a double helix pattern reminiscent of the shape of the DNA molecule. John

Michell has described Hermes as the mercurial deity that 'hovers above the old paths and standing stones'. Thoth, meanwhile, the Egyptian version of Hermes, is remembered in the Celtic god Tout, and Britain's 'tot', 'toot' and 'tut' hills. Thoth and Hermes were both guides over pathways and journeys. Whorls of words within words.

The Caduceus.

2

The Spell of the Archetype

According to Carl Gustav Jung (1875–1961), the Swiss psychologist, it is by recognising archetypal patterns in the unconscious that a person develops towards wholeness, self-realisation and self-fulfilment. The unconscious, he said, is made up of archetypes, derived not from personal experience, but in some way inherited.

The circle, square, triangle, diamond, cross and pentagram have all exerted their symbolic influence, but it is the protean spiral which has been intuitively recognised as the most subtle and at the same time most dynamic of even these potent patterns. Geometrically unique in the way it curves towards a microcosmic infinity at one extremity, and a macrocosmic infinity at the opposite extremity, its special movement signifies the one constant factor in the universe: change.

Although Jung's first career choice was archaeology, he went on to study medicine at the University of Basel. While working under the neurologist Krafft-Ebing, he settled on psychiatry as his vocation. After graduating, he took a post at a mental hospital in Zurich under Eugene Bleuler, an expert on schizophrenia, the name he gave to the condition. In 1903, Jung married Emma Rauschenbach. He taught at the University of Zurich, ran a private practice, and invented the technique of word association.

An admirer of Freud (1856–1939), Jung met him in Vienna in 1907. It is said that when they met, Freud cancelled his appointments for the day, and they talked for 13 hours, such was this convergence of two great minds. Freud came to see Jung as the crown prince of psychoanalysis and his heir apparent, but Jung had never been fully committed to Freud's theories and their relationship began to cool in 1909 while they were on a trip to America together.

World War I was a painful period of self-examination for Jung, but also marked the advent of one of the most persuasive theories of personality ever put forward. After the war, Jung travelled widely, visiting Africa, America, and India. He retired in 1946, avoiding public attention after Emma died in 1955.

In the Jungian use of the term, archetypes are the distilled memories of the human species, and they arise from the common experience of all mankind. They cannot be easily represented in verbal terms but rather by elusive symbols which, for example, have been shared by all mythologies.

Archetypal forms are not just static patterns but living, dynamic factors and, as much found as invented, they exert a 'spell' or fascination. The archetype is not an idea which is inherited but, said Jung, 'an inherited tendency of the human mind to form representations of mythological motifs – representations that vary a great deal without losing their basic pattern'. This inherited tendency is instinctive.

Jung thought that archetypes were without known origin, that they existed not just in individuals, nor in mankind as a whole, but in some kind of continuum outside space and time. Such a continuum – or pleroma, a Gnostic term denoting the eternal realm outside the world of temporal existence – evidently has allowed spirality to be prevalent throughout the whole of nature. As an archetypal pattern, or imprint, it seems to go considerably further back than even the origin of myths, beyond the primeval ocean, beyond the cooling gas and dust clouds which became the solar system, into intergalactic space itself long before the Earth was created.

Meaning, with the advent of consciousness in humans, was gradually intuited, and the symbol itself engendered a numinous experience involving that all-pervasive sense of a dependence upon the Other, that 'otherworldliness', which is unapproachable and awesome, and yet captivating at the same time.

With, as Jung said, all archetypes possessing a positive, favourable, bright side pointing upwards, and a negative, unfavourable and dark side pointing downwards, one could almost say the spiral is the 'archetypal archetype'.

At the unconscious level, humankind is in touch with the cosmic forces of nature – indeed, Jung stated that the human unconscious 'strives to fill the illimitable emptiness of space'. It is by activating the archetypal symbol that we acquire those extraordinary powers frequently described as 'magical'. Indeed, the recognition of the meaning and potency of the spiral pattern as a divine mark or signature on nature can be deemed theurgical in character and, by means of ritual, itself having become archetypal, capable of invoking beneficent 'spirits'.

Such powers lie behind the efforts and achievements of the ancient megalith builders of western Europe and of the Pyramids of Egypt, the practisers of *feng shui* in China, the watchers of the 'dragon' or creation paths among the Australian aborigines and the North American indians, and the designers of the great geometrical patterns of the Peruvian Nasca plains.

I have little doubt that Jung's archetypes hold the key to understanding the esoteric meanings of a great deal of the annals of mythology and ritual around the world which have come down to us. It tends to explain why so many of the sacred writings and traditions of ancient civilisations render themselves so puzzling and obscure to the uninitiated. It must be because, to a great extent, the archetypes, whether pictorial or linguistic, find recognition in the intuitive right-brain which contains the route to the personal and the collective unconscious, and not in the logical left-brain.

Jung found that he had to pore over old texts and delve into ancient cultures and many esoteric traditions to gain an understanding of the problems which patients brought him, and an explanation of their psychic development. In this, he took a hermeneutic approach.

Hermeneutics was a term first used in the 17th century to signify the principles and methods needed to interpret the meaning of the Bible, and later extended to embrace not only sacred texts but any written text, and 'beyond that the whole sphere of human symbolic expression' (J J Clarke, *Jung and Eastern Thought*, 1994). The 'hermeneutic circle', namely, the process whereby a series of comparisons between the narrow and the wider context progressively illuminates the individual text or symbol, is better understood as a spiral, for the circle, in actuality, can never be closed, but turns on itself endlessly. It is this spiral progression which, according to Clarke, 'represents the core of the methodology through which he (Jung) sought to establish the universal characteristics of the collective unconscious'.

Jung, in discussing the goal of human wholeness, or self-actualisation, to which the psychotherapeutic process is directed, said: 'The way to the goal seems chaotic and interminable at first, and only gradually do the signs increase that it is leading anywhere. The way is not straight but appears to go round in circles. More accurate knowledge has proved it to go in spirals: the dream-motifs always return after certain intervals to definite forms, whose characteristic it is to define a centre. And as a matter of fact the whole process revolves about a central point or some arrangement round a centre... As manifestations of unconscious processes, the dreams rotate or circumambulate round the centre, drawing closer to it as the amplifications increase in distinctness and scope... the process of development proves on closer inspection to be cyclic or spiral. We might draw a parallel between such spiral courses and the processes of growth in plants...' ('Psychology and Alchemy', Collected Works, vol. 12).

The spiral nature of this development, or 'individuation', to use the term Jung applied to it, is induced by the complementarity of past and future, expressed in his concept of 'regressive renaissance', the idea that we cannot simply move forward, but can do so only by locating a symbol from our past in order to transform. The dynamic progression of the actualisation of the Self is thus a complex process.

One finds a concrete example of the kind of spiral progression that Jung envisages in Karen Armstrong's book, 'The Spiral Staircase' (2004). A former nun who left her teaching order in 1969 after seven years of hoping but finally failing to find enlightenment, Karen knew almost nothing about the secular world she was entering. She found herself suffering from panic attacks and strange seizures, and her attempts to find happiness and succeed at a career seemed doomed to failure. After a series of fresh starts and disappointing setbacks, she realised she was trying to raise herself out of a darkness. Eventually diagnosed with epilepsy and obtaining proper treatment, she began the writing career that would turn out to be her true calling.

She describes her spiritual journey in terms of a spiral movement, and takes the image of the poet 'painfully climbing' a spiral staircase in T S Eliot's 'Ash Wednesday'. She says: 'This image is reflected in the twisting sentences of the verse, which often revolves upon itself, repeating the same words and phrases, apparently making little headway, but pushing steadily forwards nevertheless. My own life has progressed in the same way ... I was slowly climbing out of the darkness.'

Jung also said: 'What is particularly noteworthy ... is the consistent development of the central symbol. We can hardly escape the feeling that the unconscious process moves spiral-wise round a centre, gradually getting closer, while the characteristics of the centre grow more and more distinct... Accordingly, we often find spiral representations of the centre, as for instance the serpent coiled round the creative point, the egg.' (Ibid, p217). And in 'The Structure and Dynamics of the Self' in 'Aion', Jung showed that the images of quaternities of the Self seemed to represent a spiral movement.

'It remains forever itself but simultaneously it produces a higher level of consciousness. One could describe this movement as a spiral-shaped chain of quaternities which circumambulate an unchanging centre, at the same time rising each time to a higher level.'

Barbara Hannah (1891–1986), *Jung: his life and work*, 1977

When we probe a little more deeply below the surface of the psyche, Jung pointed out, we come upon historical layers which are far from otiose but active and alive in all of us, perhaps even to an extent that we are unable to imagine in the present state of our knowledge. And yet, Jung certainly did not overlook the significance of the meaning of the spiral itself which, above all patterns or symbols, stands for the unity or one-ness of the cosmos.

He also referred to the magic circle, or mandala, which, because of the protection it implied, he thought could be a form of mother archetype, appearing in an almost infinite variety of aspects, including those things and places which stood for fertility and fruitfulness. Jung made a revealing study of mandala symbolism in which the spiral appears in many different guises; the presence of the spiral as one of the basic elements of mandalas, derived from dreams, the imagination and 'individual fantasy', provides striking evidence of its prevalence in the collective unconscious.

Mandala is a Sanskrit word meaning 'circle', and is the Indian term for circles drawn in religious rituals. Some of the most elaborate and significant of mandalas are to be found in Tibetan Buddhism, and the method is also used in the Chinese I Ching. Mandalas are instruments of meditation and concentration, designed for the purpose of realising inner experience. Jung said they also expressed the idea of a safe refuge, of inner reconciliation and wholeness, and were an expression of the self. He also believed that mandalas could take the form of a ritual dance or temple building which might be connected with a sacred place.

Stupas – large mounds found throughout south-east Asia, originally built to house sacred relics – can be seen as three-dimensional versions of the mandala, conveying the symbolism of wholeness and cosmic spiritual integration, and acting as objects of mental concentration as the devotee proceeds on a spiral pathway leading upwards to enlightenment. Erection of a *stupa* was presented as one of the chief means of attaining Buddhahood.

In Tantric yoga, *kundalini* – the Sanskrit word for 'spiral' and which also suggests 'serpent power' – rises through the body through a series of seven energy centres, or *chakras*, the aim being to activate this spiritual and psychic energy by using various yogic techniques, and raise it from the lowest to the highest *chakra*. *Kundalini* is often depicted as a coiled serpent. The upward spiralling of the *kundalini* serpent symbolised, according to Jung, 'the urge of realisation (which) naturally pushes man on to be himself'. (Psychological Commentary on Kundalini Yoga, part 1, 'Spring: a journal of archetypal psychology and Jungian thought', 1975). For Jung, this involved the full realisation of the Self, through the natural and universal process of individuation, by which a person is existentially formed and differentiated. This work of becoming fully human, assisted by the will, is the work of the whole personality, embracing the Self, and of which the conscious ego is only a small and vulnerable component.

The seven chakras of Kundalini yoga.

In the mandalas which Jung took from eastern mysticism, as well as those drawn by his patients, the spiral is interpreted as representing a snake symbolising, in turn, the unconscious, the 'creation of the world of forms', the process of becoming conscious of one's instinctual nature, and the guardian of treasure located at a centre hard to attain. The serpent in the guise of the dragon, as Jung pointed out, was itself a powerful archetype, especially when connected with the hero who has to vanquish it. In ancient times, the snake sometimes also personified the spinal ganglia and spinal cord.

> 'Psychologically, the serpent is the principle of *gnosis*, knowledge or emerging consciousness. The serpent's temptation represents the urge to self-realisation in man and symbolises the principle of individuation. Some gnostic sects even identified the serpent in the Garden of Eden with Christ.'

Edward F Edinger (1922–98), *Ego and Archetype*, 1992

Of particular interest is Jung's account of a young girl who at times of stress drew pictures with a mandala structure which were 'magic circles' – intended to stop the difficulties of the outside world from entering her mind, and representing a form of self-protection. In another case, Jung remarks upon four 'eddies' in a subject's painting which are, in actuality, four spirals forming a quaternity, the quaternity itself being an archetypal image common to mandalas and, indeed, having always existed, especially in the form of the cross.

Barbara Hannah, who was a psychotherapist, analyst and teacher at the C G Jung Institute in Switzerland, tells how Jung analysed a dream, in 1929, which involved a steamroller in a wood, not making a straight road but 'an intricate pattern in two rhythms which, looked at, as the dreamer did, from above, turned out to be a square. Inside it, at the centre, was a spiral footpath leading to the centre of all'. This led to Jung telling his pupils a great deal about mandalas, not only in the Chinese parallel on which he was working at the time, but many others from all over the world which his investigations had uncovered.

Jung thought it probable that, in general, a leftward rotation in the 'eddy', or spiral, indicated movement towards the unconscious, while a rightward or clockwise rotation moved towards consciousness. The leftward turning spiral spins into the unconscious, while the right-turning spiral spins out of unconscious chaos.

'The Descent into the Maelstrom' by Edgar Allan Poe (1809–49), can be read as an allegory of this idea. A giant whirlpool off the coast of Norway is referred to in medieval and Renaissance chronicles, and in Norse mythology the Maelstrom was believed to be the route to the world of the dead, a conduit by means of which the worlds of the dead and the living were connected.

Poe, born in Boston, Massachusetts, to parents who were itinerant actors, started his writing career as a staff member of various magazines.

His first collection, 'Tales of the Grotesque and Arabesque', appeared in 1840, and contained one of his most famous works, 'The Fall of the House of Usher'. Poe suffered from bouts of depression and madness, and attempted suicide in 1848. In the following year, he overdosed on opium following an argument with his fiancee's mother, and died a few months later after being found collapsed in a Baltimore gutter.

In 'The Descent into the Maelstrom' (1841), a fisherman's boat is caught in a violent hurricane and sucked into the 'great whirlpool of the Maelstrom' – a monstrous mile-wide vortex spinning to the right. As the boat is drawn into the 'abyss of the whirl', the full moon breaks through cloud, casting a ghastly light on the awesome scene. The fisherman, by observing the movement of debris in the flow of the whirlpool, as his boat races along on the wall of water, sees that large objects are rapidly consigned to the depths, while smaller ones are not, and that of these smaller objects, spherical ones disappear quickly while cylindrical ones hold their position.

The fisherman lashes himself to a cask and throws himself overboard, while his boat spirals down into oblivion below him (taking his brother with it). The cask sinks little before the 'whirl of the Strom' abates, and the fisherman is lifted to the surface, and saved. Appropriately, the moon is now setting 'radiantly' in the west.

Poe intuitively decided to describe a right-turning whirlpool, or eddy, the 'world of ocean we had left' being to larboard of the fishing boat, and starboard being 'next the whirl'. Like Poe's fisherman, we move away from 'unconscious chaos', towards the goal of increased consciousness, by understanding the significance of events in the turn of the spiral. Although terrifying, the right-turning Strom offered a means of salvation in the midst of utmost adversity, that balance of opposites which, when embraced, can provide a glimpse of the soul, which is the basis of existence.

At the same time, the descent into the maelstrom may be seen as representing a confrontation with the unconscious in the search for totality of self, the goal of psychic development. Crucially, Jung said that there was no linear evolution in this development, in the process of individuation, but only circumambulation of the Self.

'The Descent into the Maelstrom' is surely also a version of the archetypal 'night sea journey', the ancient legend of the hero swallowed by an enormous fish, or whale, as in the Biblical story of Job, or as recounted in the story of Odysseus' descent into the Underworld. It is so-called because the tale is associated with the sun sinking in the west and journeying under the sea to rise at dawn in the east. The journey involves a withdrawal from life, into a kind of womb, and then rebirth into the world – it is significant that the central character of Poe's story is a fisherman, a character which has close associations with the Christ image. Certainly, the night sea journey, or Nekyia, was one of the main organising myths in Jung's works. In order to achieve psychic wholeness, he thought, each individual had to go on such a journey, that symbolic re-enactment of the rising and setting of the sun. The journey is necessary because it is only by re-entering the mother, in the form of the belly of the whale or some chthonic region, that the hero can achieve spiritual rebirth.

Joseph Campbell, the American scholar of mythology and comparative religion, believed that myths such as these have a direct relevance to the individual's life experience, and act as a source of inspirational guidance for everyday living. He was fond of referring to 'the journey of the hero', the battle which, at some time or other in our lives, we all have to wage against obstacles, even 'powers of darkness'. He believed that human beings all share the same gods, are informed by the same archetypes, and that the natural forces that animate us are common and divine.

Campbell (1904–87), born in White Plains, New York, to Catholic middle-class parents, immersed himself in Native American culture, and it could be said that his outlook was shaped by the conjunction of the two mythological worldviews. After earning a BA from Columbia, and receiving an MA for his work in Arthurian studies, he was awarded a travelling fellowship to continue his studies at the University of Paris. Later he moved to the University of Munich and it was during this period that he came into contact with doyens of modernism, notably, the sculptor Antoine Bourdelle, Pablo Picasso, Paul Klee, James Joyce, Thomas Mann, Freud and Jung, whose art and insights would greatly influence his own work. These encounters eventually led Campbell to theorise that all myths are the creative products of the human psyche, that artists are a culture's mythmakers, and that mythologies are creative manifestations of humankind's universal need to explain psychological, social, cosmological and spiritual realities.

His first major solo authorial undertaking, 'The Hero with a Thousand Faces' (1949), was published to acclaim and brought him the first of numerous awards and honours. In this study of the myth of the hero, Campbell posits the existence of a 'monomyth' (a word he borrowed from James Joyce), a universal pattern which is the essence of, and common to, heroic tales in every culture. While outlining the basic stages of this mythic cycle, he also explored common variations in the

28

hero's journey which, he argues, is an operative metaphor, not only for an individual, but for a culture as well.

Campbell urges us to explore the myths that touch us most profoundly, for these archetypal tales and legends will help us to enrich our paths through life. He wanted us to see through life metaphorically and to celebrate the myths as if they are alive in us, so as to obtain deeper insights into ourselves.

These ideas have found their way into what has come to be described today as 'sacred psychology', which seeks ways of expanding everyday consciousness by finding the means of introducing archetypal mythic options to it. One exponent is the American humanistic psychologist Dr Jean Houston, a follower of Campbell's work who, with her husband Dr Robert Masters, is a co-director of the Foundation for Mind Research. As a researcher in human capacities, Houston, together with Masters, has focused on the understanding of latent human abilities. She is the founder of the Mystery School, an existential programme of cross-cultural mythic and spiritual studies dedicated to teaching history, philosophy, the new physics, psychology, anthropology, myth, and the many dimensions of human potential.

Houston sees archetypes as bridging spirit with nature, mind and body, and self with universe. In her 'The Hero and the Goddess' (1992), the first book in her Transforming Myths series, she says: 'They (the archetypes) are always within us, essential structures within the structure of our psyches.' An important aspect of sacred psychology is to assist the individual in transforming his or her life from the 'person-particular' to the 'personal-universal', thereby providing day-to-day living with a new vision.

Under the classic Jungian approach, elements of the self often reveal themselves as opposites wrapped up in each other: emotionality/rationality, happiness/sadness, intimacy/distance, for example. The ideal is to achieve a marriage of opposites, a reconciliation of contraries, within the individual, to allow him or her to become creative and vitally alive. Jung used the term of the Ancient Greeks, 'hieros gamos', or sacred marriage, to describe this mystical union.

'We are crucified between the opposites and delivered up to the torture until the reconciling third takes shape,' he said. This 'reconciling third' is the innermost region of the psyche, the organising centre which includes the ego but is not in any way defined by it, a transpersonal, transcendent reality that Jung called the Self. His view was that we have to be 'crucified with Christ' – for Christ is the nearest analogy of self and its meaning – and hang suspended in a state of moral suffering, undergoing the experience of a metaphorical crucifixion which can be as terrifying as being confronted by the whirling waters of the Maelstrom, and which promises salvation and destruction simultaneously.

> **Jungian analyst Edward F Edinger refers to Jung's discovery that the archetypal psyche has a structuring or ordering principle which unifies the various archetypal contents – the central archetype, or archetype of wholeness, which Jung termed the Self. The Self is the ordering and unifying centre of the total psyche (conscious and unconscious) as the ego is the centre of conscious personality. 'The process of alternation between ego-Self union and ego-Self separation seems to occur repeatedly throughout the life of the individual both in childhood and in maturity. Indeed, this cyclic (or better, spiral) formula seems to express the basic process of psychological development from birth to death.'**

Edinger, *Ego and Archetype,* 1972

In nature, both left- and right-handed spirals are found, just as virtually every elementary particle has an anti-particle of equal but opposite charge. Yet, particularly at the microscopic level, right-handed or clockwise-turning spirals seem to be favoured by nature (just as right-handedness is favoured in humans).

If these spirals do indeed turn towards an ordered continuum then it is possibly not surprising that they are to be found in those organisms which have been equipped for survival, and that we tend to perceive an ordered universe.

It is not yet known whether the universe is inherently near-symmetrical in this way – matter being more abundant than anti-matter – or whether there is perfect symmetry with 'mirror images' of everything, despite the fact that the discovery of anti-particles implies anti-people, anti-planets and even anti-universes!

The comparative rarity of left-handed spirals has led them to be looked upon as having enhanced magical qualities, apparently due at least in part to the fact that anyone traversing a left-handed spiral path towards its centre moves in the direction of the apparent clockwise move-ment of the sun across the sky. This direction has influenced various customs, both sacred and secular, the opposite direction having been considered unlucky – as in taking an anti-clockwise path 'widdershins' (which means 'against the sun') around a church.

The people of Travancore, India, believed that the sacred shell, *sankho*, was a manifestation of the god Vishnu because its internal spiral pattern does not turn to the right, as do millions of other such shells, but to the left. This *turbinella rapa*, known as the 'chank shell', appears in Hindu religious art held in the hand of Vishnu, while Shiva in Hindu myth holds a spiral nautilus shell as a symbol of an instrument of creation. Moreover, such shells, conches, have been used ritualistically as ornaments, and even as currency, by peoples all over the world, some since extremely early times. In Taoist thought, movement to the right represents a 'falling' life process embodying the feminine or *yin* principle, while leftward motion means the 'rising' movement of life incorporating the masculine or *yang* principle.

Conclusions which Jung drew from his work with mandalas, and his ideas on the rotation of spirals, dovetail neatly with such perceptions. Indeed, many of Jung's central ideas find powerful echoes in the traditions of Western magic and esoterica, where the idea of personal spiritual advancement through self-knowledge, initiation and rites of passage is prominent. The process which Jung called individuation finds a counterpart in the Kabbalistic Tree of Life where the archetype of Tiphareth, standing for the Sun, symbolises spiritual rebirth and wholeness, and acts as an intermediary between man and God on the ascent towards Heaven. Occultists have always endeavoured to explore the visionary nature of inner being, and their rituals and formulae were designed to bring the gods into consciousness.

Jung actually likened the 'secret of individuation' to the Holy Grail, saying it was a mystery and that human comprehension simply ended there. As a boy, he had studied the Grail legends and learned them by heart and, in 1920, while in England to give a series of talks in Cornwall, he and his wife Emma visited Glastonbury and Tintagel to look for Grail sites. Indeed, Emma made the study of the Grail legends her life's work, and went on to write a book about them, showing that they cast light on the search for the ultimate value of life, and for what makes our lives most meaningful. As a living myth which remains of tremendous relevance to modern times, one might say it is the Grail that lies at the centre of the individuation spiral, that elusive treasure wrapped in the coils of a serpent-dragon at the heart of the winding labyrinth.

'In Jungian analysis, we repeatedly find that we have arrived at the same spots, but each time on a higher level, as Jung expresses it – the way to individuation being like a spiral up which we climb.'

Barbara Hannah, *Encounters with the Soul: active imagination as developed by C G Jung*, 1981

31

3

Ritual, Art and Nature

'A figure with curves always offers a lot of interesting angles.'

Mae West (1892–1980)

It is clear that throughout history the spiral has held a deep, sigilistic fascination for humankind, its prevalence in nature being mirrored in ritual and art down to the present day, always reflecting the acute human sensitivity towards, and recognition of, patterns. This propensity seems to have been hard-wired into the human genome during our evolutionary millennia, indicating that it is there for a very good reason. Originally, perhaps, as human consciousness dawned, there was a need to perceive order in a hostile and unpredictable environment, and patterns which were perceived to be enduring and recurring, such as the spiral, would have become the bearers of an alluring mystery and the promise of a profound meaning.

The spiral is found represented in cultures all over the globe, from Stone Age societies in Europe and the Near East 15000–10000BC, and pre-dynastic Egypt c4500BC, to the Kansu settlements of China 2500–2000BC, at Chavin de Huantar in Peru 900–200BC, and throughout the history of Polynesian and Maori communities in the Pacific, to cite only a few examples.

Chinese archaeologists discovered more than 700 stone discs connected with 12,000-year-old burial sites in the Baian Kara Ula mountains near the Tibetan border, each one engraved with a spiral of pictograms yet to be satisfactorily translated.

Similarly, the enigmatic Phaistos Disc, made of baked clay and thought to date from about 1,700BC, and so named after it was found in the ancient city of Phaistos in southern Crete (although it possibly originated in Egypt or the Middle East), bears a spiral of as yet undeciphered pictograms on each side.

The Towie ball, dated to 3000BC, found in Aberdeenshire.

At Skara Brae, the neolithic 'Pompeii' of Orkney, a stone ball carved with a spiral ornament was found. To archaeologists, the function of this ball, like that of other similar ones discovered in northern Scotland, is unknown. It has been suggested that their makers had connections with the Boyne valley of Ireland where similar art has been found.

Beautiful interlocking spirals ornament a carved stone ball – the Towie ball, dated to 3000BC – which was discovered at Glaschul Hill, Upper Donside, Aberdeenshire. Stone Age pendulums used for dowsing, found in Irish temple cairns, have spiral engravings. Mycenaean influences on early Bronze Age art in Europe were, in particular, spiral and triskele ornamental motifs. Three spirals comprised the 'triskelion' which was also a common Celtic magical symbol.

> 'Nothing in this world remains unchanged but for one moment only. Everything changes aspect, it dissolves, merges with other elements and displays a new aspect, different from the previous one.'
>
> *Heraclitus (c540–475BC)*

Ionic columns are characterised by the spiral volutes of their capitals, this order of architecture being named after Ionia, the ancient district of the Mediterranean and the Aegean where a school of philosophy developed about 2,500 years ago. The leading light of the Ionian group of philosophers was Heraclitus, a Greek philosopher of the late sixth century BC who lived at Ephesus on the Ionian coast of Asia Minor, who can be said to be the founder of metaphysics, and who dealt in fundamental occult precepts.

It is not surprising that the spiral came to be a key symbol in Ionic architecture – and was used in a form which was in harmony with the lines of organic growth – when one discovers, for instance, that Heraclitus, known as 'the Obscure', or the 'dark philosopher', was the first to put the problem of change and order at the centre of a philosophical system. He complained that men failed to understand the 'logos', that universal element of things in accordance with which all natural events and human behaviour must proceed.

For Heraclitus, the physical world was a place of change, but change regulated by, and endowed with, a kind of unity by the 'logos'. Most of these changes he envisaged as between opposites, and he tried to show how men's souls and behaviour were essentially connected with the world as a whole, and in this he made philosophical advances of great importance. Echoes of his thinking are found in Taoist philosophy, in the I Ching, and even in the descriptions which quantum physics gives to events in the sub-atomic world.

His philosophy is perhaps also more fundamental in the formation of the European mind than any other thinker in European history, including Socrates, Plato and Aristotle. This is because Heraclitus, like Parmenides, postulated a model of nature and the universe which created the foundation for all other speculation on physics and metaphysics. He criticised other thinkers who failed to see the unity of experience. Opposites are essential, he says, but they are unified in a system of balanced exchanges. The world is identified with an ongoing process governed by a law of change, and the underlying law of nature also manifests itself as a moral law for people. Heraclitus was the first Western philosopher to look beyond physical theory to search for metaphysical foundations and moral applications.

Herbert Weaver, in *Divining the Primary Sense: unfamiliar radiation in nature, art and science*, 1978, explains how early man used the spiral symbol to invite the sympathy and beneficence of a fertility god and, sometimes in pairs, to afford protection against dangerous external forces. He termed these symbolic designs 'magneto-protective' devices.

Ritual triggers the imaginative processes, and has strong symbolic elements, and in ancient times it was frequently devised to accompany important turning points in the lives of individuals, or in the experiences of whole communities, at moments which were naturally liminal, and which often involved issues of birth, death and rebirth. 'Without rituals we may as well be dead,' Confucius remarked.

Theodore Andrea Cook (of whom more later) made the first detailed excursions into the subject of spirals in nature and art at the turn of the 19th century, and he realised early in his studies that the spiral had for long been associated with escape from danger, as well as with ascent into new being. At the baptism of a Lithuanian child, the parents buried one of his or her curls so that the child might 'twine out of danger' in life, as the spiral tendrils of the plant twined upwards to the light. Similarly, by the 'doctrine of signatures', certain races used the twisted seed pods of the tropical *helicteres ixora* as medicine for 'twisted bowels', or colic.

In Babylonian magic, which went into decline after the Islamic conquest 1,000 years ago, incantation bowls, with spells inscribed in a spiral inside, were used by sorcerers to deflect evil from those who consulted them, and such artefacts are still being discovered in Iraq today.

> **'The seemingly endless repetition of visual phrases upon the stones of the Western Atlantic shows that this style of megalithic art was meant to be employed as a meditational device in the manner that we moderns use music such as reggae.'**
>
> Julian Cope, *The Megalithic European*, 2004

Paired or triple spirals are found carved on the walls of prehistoric burial chambers, such as at Newgrange in the Boyne valley in Ireland, and at Gavrinis in the Carnac area of Brittany, and on grave stelae such as those unearthed at Mycenae, dating from 1500BC. They are also to be found carved on the neolithic temples at Tarxien and Hagar Qim in Malta, and in the Orkneys at Eday Manse and on the Westray stone, which was reassembled after being found in pieces at Pierowall quarry and is now in the visitor centre at Maeshowe.

At Newgrange, above the entranceway of the mound, is a 'roof box' which allows the dawn sun at the winter solstice to strike into an inner chamber and illuminate three linked spirals cut into the wall. Stone carvings on this monument feature mainly spirals and circles, but also serpentine shapes and zigzags.

The entrance stone, in particular, which has been described as the most remarkable example of megalithic art in western Europe, is engraved with a complex pattern of spirals, concentric arcs and diamond shapes. The overall structure is believed to have been covered at one time with shining white quartz, for scores of white pebbles were

35

The entrance stone at the prehistoric chamber tomb at Newgrange in the Boyne Valley in Ireland.

collected there by Professor M J O'Kelly, of University College, Cork, during investigations of the site. The spirals of the entrance stone are reflected on a beautifully carved and polished solid flint macehead found at Knowth in County Meath and which is regarded as another outstanding work of neolithic craftsmanship, evidently achieved only by the action of stone and sand on stone.

Shapes similar to those at Newgrange, including a spiral, are carved at the Barclodiad-y-Gawres passage grave on Anglesey, and at Bryn Celli Ddu, an earth-covered passage mound there, dating from about 3500BC and orientated to the changing seasons, the summer solstice sunrise filling the passage with light which is reflected from a quartz surface to illuminate a spiral carved on an area of stone near the entrance.

'The double and triple spirals on the entrance stone to Newgrange swirl and flow like the starry sky itself. They not only evoke the motion of the waves at sea but the serpentine energies of the earth itself.'

Peter Marshall, *Europe's Lost Civilisation: uncovering the mysteries of the megaliths*, 2004

'...the Irish knots and spirals, images that go back thousands of years, showing the complexities and

circularities of every human life. Modern science prefers the
straight line of evolution as the energetic principle. The Irish
spirals complement the Taoist idea that a thing is always
entangled with its opposite: yin always looping into yang.'

Thomas Moore, *Dark Nights of the Soul*, 2004

On the other side of the world, in the American Southwest, a 1,000-
year-old Anasazi summer solstice marker sends a shaft of sunlight
between upright stone slabs to bisect a spiral etched into a rock face. At
the winter solstice, this same calendrical device creates a sliver of sunlight
on either side of the spiral. The mechanism was graphically demonstrated
by Carl Sagan in his 1981 television series 'Cosmos'. Another Anasazi
petroglyph, south of Albuquerque, depicts the Morning Star god next
to a coiled snake in the form of a spiral.

An adobe frieze in the Uhle compound at Chan Chan in Peru, the
imperial capital in the Andean empire of Chimor 1,000 years ago, shows a
series of beautiful wave volutes indicating veneration of the sea. The spiral
is commonly found in examples of earlier Moche Valley art too.

More than 700 years ago, at the Holly House site at the Hovenweep
National Monument, on the border of Utah and Colorado, Anasazi

An Anasazi spiral rock carving in the American Southwest.

dwellers marked the changing seasons too. Two huge boulders form a narrow corridor open to the eastern horizon; the western end is blocked by another large boulder, and on the southern side of the corridor a number of petroglyphs are cut — two spirals and the typical Pueblo sun symbol of three concentric circles with a central dot. At the summer solstice sunrise, a narrow beam of sunlight enters the corridor and cuts across one of the spirals, and then, as it elongates, reaches the other. A second serpent of light then cuts the sun symbol close to its centre.

A paired spiral pin was found at Cadbury Castle, Somerset, one of the suggested locations of King Arthur's Camelot, and dated to about 750BC. Several silver spiral rings were found by 19th century antiquarians who excavated the Anglo-Saxon burial ground at Chessell Down on the Isle of Wight. One such ring was still on the finger of a skeleton.

An interesting theory for the origin of the double spiral design is put forward by masonic researchers Christopher Knight and Robert Lomas in their book 'Uriel's Machine: the ancient origin of science'. Lomas gained a first class honours degree in electrical engineering before turning to research into solid state physics, later working on guidance systems for Cruise missiles and becoming involved in the early development of personal computers. Knight has a degree in advertising and graphic design, and is a consumer psychologist concerned with the planning of new products and their marketing.

In their book, they describe an important discovery by the American artist Charles Ross who, after receiving a BA in mathematics in 1960 and an MA in sculpture in 1962 from the University of California, Berkeley, began experimenting with large-scale prisms to project large bands of solar colour into buildings. He creates arrays of giant prisms specifically geared to the sun and mounted in skylights, the spectra always changing due to the turning of the Earth.

Ross's inspiration was to use a lens to direct the sun's rays onto a wooden plank so that it burned a track as it moved overhead. He positioned a new plank each day and, over a period of 366 days, the pattern created was a double spiral. In the summer, it was a compact right-handed spiral, and in the winter, a more open left-handed one — an intriguing contrast, if one thinks of the right-turning spiral moving towards consciousness (the brightness of summer), and the left-turning one towards the unconscious (the darkness of winter).

At the equinoxes, the track straightened out as the loose winter spiral ended and was turned into a compact spiral turning in the opposite direction. Each spiral represented a quarter of the sun's movement across the sky. In 1993 – 'The Year Of Solar Burns' – Ross was commissioned by the French Ministry of Culture to provide a permanent installation in the 15th century Chateau d'Oiron in the Loire Valley.

Another remarkable project of Ross's, in 1994–96, was his collaboration with Virginia Dwan and architect Laban Wingert to create the Dwan Light Sanctuary, a circular chamber at the United World College in Montezuma, New Mexico, where the dimensions and sloping walls of the structure are based on astronomical alignments. Twenty-four large prisms produce orchestrated spectra, changing by the hour and with the seasons. A square window frames the Pole Star.

Knight and Lomas also found that two poles placed in the ground a few feet apart will trace a spiral shadow as the sun moves outward from the spring equinox, and retrace it to the starting point for the autumn equinox. After that, it moves back to create a spiral in the opposite direction, before returning to the starting point. A single spiral equals three months, and a full year is represented by a 'figure-of-eight' double spiral covered twice over.

The authors speculate that the megalith builders used this seminal solar spiral to represent the quarter-year, as at Bryn Celli Ddu. They extrapolate from this that the triple spirals of Newgrange represent the human gestation period of nine months, or three-quarters of the year, and that the monument was therefore a 'birthing chamber' and not a tomb – we have already noted how spirality is related to the archetypes of birth and rebirth. However, as one might expect, the naturally occurring spirals created by Ross's lens and the pole shadows of Knight and Lomas are rudimentary and have none of the stylised elegance of many of the Neolithic carvings, the origins of which, I believe, are to be found much deeper in the human psyche.

In Egypt, spirally-formed seashells were regarded as protection against evil forces, and a vital sign. Australian aborigines still erect alignments of small stones terminating in spirals or loops, and which are associated with ancestral beings and the replenishment of living creatures.

In Ken Russell's 1983 film interpretation of Holst's *Planets Suite*, the sequence for Neptune, the Mystic, opens with an aborigine tracing a spiral in the sand with his finger. In an inspired leap, this scene cuts to a shot of a man climbing a ladder up to the dish of a radio telescope, followed by another showing three people traversing the gyres of an initiatory pavement labyrinth.

39

The value given in the East to the lotus – itself a symbol of creative power or energy, of primeval emergence, of the strength and divinity of the sun, and of many sacred phenomena, as well as a body position for meditation – is probably due to its association with the spiral pattern. The eye of the Buddha is shaped in Eastern art in the form of a lotus petal. Similarly, the lotus is related to any of the various water lilies, including several represented in Ancient Egyptian and Hindu art and religious symbolism.

Symbolising the 'dragon current' in the earth, which various investigators believe to be transmitted across land and water by leys, the spiral is the natural emblem of the ancient art of geomancy, a word taken from the Greek and meaning literally 'earth divination'. Geomancy deals with the integration of humans and their undertakings with their natural surroundings, and is practised in two distinct forms, divinatory and telluric. The dictionary describes geomancy as 'divination from a figure given by a handful of earth thrown down, or from figures given by dots made at random', and this was the form in which geomancy made its first appearance, its roots being in Arabia and Africa.

In some respects resembling the 3,000-year-old Chinese I Ching method of divination, geomancy took its place alongside astrology and the Tarot as a pre-eminent means of foretelling the future. Divinatory geomancy can be defined as the art of achieving special insight into the future, or the present, by studying the relationships between patterns made in the earth, or on paper, by a person allowing his or her intuition, or 'earth spirits', to guide the marker.

Telluric geomancy, meanwhile, concerns the concentration of earth energies and the proper positioning of holy sites and monuments, frequently to reflect the sacred geometry of the universe. Evidence of its influence on the landscape and on architecture can be found all over the world. The Chinese art of *feng shui*, for example, involves the tracing of 'dragon veins' in the landscape which contain the earth energy, or *ch'i*, to determine the most beneficial places for building, or for burying the dead. This type of geomancy took account of cosmology, astronomy, religion, astrology and numerology, and it flourished several thousand years ago.

The spiral, supremely meaningful among the patterns welling up through the human psyche in dreams and visions, recognised and incorporated in an accurate reading of natural phenomena, and suggestive of swirling cosmic energy, was indispensable in bringing about a practice which, on a global scale, was the confluence of many disciplines and everywhere consistent in its purpose and effect.

The spiral is the symbol of the motivation behind the practice of geomancy which, at different times in history, has led man to seek a proper existence in harmony with nature on a universal scale through a fusion, or orchestration, of various arts and sciences, and is present not only in the physical sense of a Jericho built in a seven-walled maze, or the design of a Renaissance 'ideal city', but in the synchronistic events of divination too.

One such art, of course, is that of dowsing, the oldest known divining rod being the *lituus*, a straight twig twisted into a spiral shape. Romulus was said to have used one of these in laying out the boundaries of Rome, and it later came to be the badge of office of the Roman pontiffs, or high priests, whose job it was to fix the calendar and arrange the correct dates and times for religious ceremonies. The spiral form of the *lituus* made it appropriate to religious use, because from time immemorial the spiral had been a universal religious symbol of the utmost importance, frequently associated with water, the location of which is often the purpose of dowsing.

Artists in both the East and the West have used the spiral, consciously or unconsciously, and often in an extremely inspirational and powerful manner, to symbolise cosmic phenomena and to stress man's inextricable involvement with them. It is indicative of the way in which structures in the universe have shaped many of our aesthetic senses. The American architect, Frank Lloyd Wright, modelled the design of the Guggenheim Museum in New York City on the chambered nautilus. Inside, visitors view art works from a spiral ramp, the idea being that they move on by degrees just as the mollusc in the shell adds to its protective chambers.

Taoist art employs spirals singly to symbolise stars and in triple form to represent heaven, earth and humankind. Dragons amid vortices of clouds and water relate to the internal and external forces affecting humans and which are united in the transformation brought about through the Taoist's 'inner alchemy'.

The Venetian Renaissance painter Giovanni Bellini produced the 'Allegory of the Shell' in which one sees not only a huge spirally-formed shell or conch, but a man emerging from it, as if in birth from the womb, with a serpent coiled about his arms. 'The Ascent of the Blessed' by Hieronymous Bosch (c1450–1516) shows human figures being assisted by angels towards the light, or Heaven, through what appears to be a spirally-formed tunnel – a famous painting which some have interpreted as a depiction of the near-death experience.

In Rembrandt's 'Philosopher with an Open Book' (1633) an elderly man is depicted sitting in a chamber next to a spiral staircase. William

Blake's painting 'Jacob's Ladder' shows angels ascending and descending a spiral staircase between earth and heaven. Vincent Van Gogh, in his extraordinary 'Starry Night' (1889) captured a deep inner experience of 'oneness' with the universe, with night-sky clouds spun into spirals, one of them forming the classic yin-yang pattern.

In 1913, Wyndham Lewis founded a group of painters called the Vorticists, from the word 'vortex', denoting a point where energy is concentrated, Vorticism being derived from Cubism and Futurism.

The spiral is also to be found in the paintings of Marc Chagall, in 'The Purim' (1917), for example. A spiral rises from Picasso's unconscious to superimpose itself on the image of the moon in his notable oil painting 'Night Fishing at Antibes' (1939). The surrealist Dutch painter M C Escher has used the spiral in his work, as in his illustration 'Sterren' ('Stars') which depicts strange creatures with spirally-formed tongues struggling free from a bizarre space/time continuum of distorted geo-metrical figures. Victor Pasmore's 'Spiral Motif in Green, Violet, Blue and Gold: the Coast of the Inland Sea' (1950) depicts a sky of churning spiral formations.

More recently, Francesco Clemente's 'Sound, Point' (1990) depicts stars caught up in two conjoined spirals, and David Hockney's water-colour, 'Maelstrom, Bodo, 2002', shows a whole series of spiral whirlpools.

'Beat a path of retreat up them spiral staircases,
Pass the tree of smoke, pass the angel with four faces,
Begging God for mercy and weepin' in unholy places.'

Bob Dylan, *Angelina*, 1981

The Renaissance genius Leonardo da Vinci (1452–1519), painter, architect, engineer, mathematician and philosopher, studied the principles of spiral formations and made sketches of their appearances in smoke, dust and water (including the curves of waves), and in flowers, grass and reeds. For him, as his biographer Charles Nicholl says, the spiral, or *coclea* (snail-shell) as Leonardo called it, was the origin of one of the great energy principles of his physics, demonstrated in his hydraulic devices and Archimedean screws. In it lay the force found in drills, propellers and turbines and, in the natural world, in tornadoes and whirlpools. The shape appears many times in Leonardo's collection of sketches for the 'Deluge', which followed his observation of swirling floodwaters, and reveals his fascination with the power of the vortex.

The forms Leonardo drew become mesmeric, says Nicholl, their curvi-linear force-fields resolving into 'mandala-like forms'.

In one manuscript, Leonardo compares the spirals of a woman's curls to the motion of a whirlpool, and in his study 'Leda and the Swan', a subject taken from mythology, plaits of the girl's hair are arranged in spirals. These studies, said Theodore Andrea Cook, led towards 'ultimate principles of construction and of growth which Leonardo did so much to discover, and which his successors are still endeavouring to grasp'.

Leonardo, who sought fundamental laws of creation which he knew existed before the earth came into being, seemed to see what the poet Gerard Manley Hopkins in the 19th century came to call the 'inscape' of living things and its manifestations in the energy spirals and whorls of natural growth. Leonardo appeared to be especially attracted by the problems of spiral formation, and Cook credited him with the design of a beautiful spiral staircase at the Chateau de Blois in Touraine – not far from Amboise where Leonardo spent the last years of his life – based on the structure of the mollusc shell *voluta vespertilio*.

According to Cook, Leonardo found spirality 'in such humble instances as the coil of the worm, the curve of the snail shell, the budding of the fern. Completed in the Ionic capital, arrested at the bending point of the acanthus leaf in the Corinthian, it became, he saw, a primal element of architectural ornament, eloquent with many meanings, representing the power of his favourite waves and winds in Greek building, typifying the old Serpent of unending Sin in Gothic workmanship'.

Thomas de Quincey (1785–1859), the English Romantic essayist and critic, best-known for his autobiographical 'Confessions of an English Opium Eater' (1821), used the term 'involute', to indicate a spiral curve, a rolling inwards of intense meaningfulness from perception of the world. Poems, said de Quincey, can speak only 'by deep impulse, by hieroglyphic suggestion. Their teaching is not direct or explicit, but lurking, implicit, masked in deep incarnations'. Such incarnations are his involutes.

Remarkably, de Quincey also referred to his prose as having a 'caduceus' style, taking the image from the intertwined serpents of the wand of the messenger god Hermes which, from antiquity, has been the symbol of the healer. De Quincey developed ·a special prose style which he regarded as soothing to emotional wounds, the sinuous and meandering course of his narrative involving a binding-up, and healing, symbolism. De Quincey's addiction to opium was life-long, and his influence on such writers as Poe and Baudelaire, as well as readers tempted to experiment with opium, was great – and infamous.

Anthropologists and evolutionary psychologists agree that, rather than being infinitely variable, human cultures are extremely similar when viewed from an appropriately abstract standpoint. Hundreds of cultural norms and practices, which must surely now include recognition of the numinosity of the spiral form, have been found to exist every-where. Universality, of course, does not necessarily prove innateness, as powerful ideas tend to spread from one culture to another; this is known as idea diffusion. However, where ideas appear not to have arisen through idea diffusion, as seems to be the case with the worldwide assimilation of the spiral pattern, universality offers a very good starting point for studies into the existence of innate traits. Although we have certainly covered a lot of ground culturally in the last 10,000 years, it's interesting to note that, in evolutionary terms, the human mind is basi-cally the same one that looked out on the African landscape where our distant ancestors were appearing more than one and a half million years ago.

It was the evolutionary biologist Professor Richard Dawkins who coined the term 'memes' for units of cultural inheritance – by analogy to genes as the units of biological inheritance – which proliferate over millennia by taking advantage of the specific nature of the human mind. Dawkins was educated at Oxford University, and taught zoology at the universities of California and Oxford. A highly esteemed scientist, he is the Charles Simonyi Professor of the Public Understanding of Science at Oxford University, and has won many awards, both scien-tific and literary, for his work, including the Humanist of the Year Award in 1996. Since then he has been vice-president of the British Humanist Association.

He proposed that the unit of cultural inheritance was naturally selected through the impact of individual characteristics on survival and replication. Some examples he gives of memes are tunes, catchphrases, fashions in clothes, ways of making pots and building arches. Dawkins stresses that the meme is not the tune, the phrase or the arch; these are just the meme's physical manifestations. The meme is the *idea* of the arch, the underlying mental representation of 'archness', and while genes have their basis in physical DNA, so memes have theirs in physical changes in the brain which occur when a person learns something. Like genes, then, memes can be inherited by successive generations.

The theory of memes reminds one of the realm of the Forms conceived by the Greek philosopher Plato (427–347BC), said to contain

44

entities existing independently of the sensible world. Plato, who some think studied in Egypt for a period, and who referred to the Egyptians as a 'race of philosophers', seems to have derived the idea from Thoth-Hermes. The 'Poimandes', the first of the ancient books of the Hermetic collection, perhaps contemporaneous with Plato although containing wisdom handed down from a much earlier period, refers to the endeavour of copying or replicating celestial perfection on Earth, and to the notion of the 'below' replicating the 'above' during the process of creation. The existence is suggested of an 'archetypal form' which can be grasped only by the mind, and which is 'prior to the beginning of things and limitless'. Moreover, the Hermetic 'Asclepius' describes a more elevated *kosmos* hidden from the senses but still influencing and shaping the lower, material or sensible world: 'If you consider the whole, you will learn that in truth the sensible *kosmos* itself, with all things that are therein, is woven like a garment by that higher *kosmos*.'

The Forms, according to Plato, are eternal patterns or 'moulds' of which everything in the material world is a poor copy, and which would include an 'ideal' arch, for example, from which all actual arches are derived. Ordinary objects are imperfect and changeable, and they copy only faintly the perfect and immutable Forms. Thus, all of the information we acquire about sensible objects is temporary, insignificant and unreliable, while genuine knowledge of the Forms themselves is perfectly certain forever. Plato argued that since we actually have knowledge of these supra-sensible realities, but knowledge that we cannot possibly have obtained through any corporeal experience, it follows that this knowledge must be a form of recollection and that our souls must have been acquainted with the Forms prior to our births. However, the existence of our mortal bodies therefore cannot be essential to the existence of our souls – before birth or after death – and we are therefore immortal.

More significantly, memes seem to have a parallel in the archetypes which, says Jung, make up the collective unconscious and which are somehow transmitted from generation to generation. We have seen how Jung thought that the archetypes were without known origin, and that they existed in a continuum outside space and time. But perhaps this is not the case. Perhaps, like memes, they arise through physical changes in the brain, triggered by experiences since the dawn of consciousness, which can then be inherited.

If we view the archetypal spiral as a memetic form we can arrive at a biological explanation for the way it has permeated human culture for thousands of years.

45

SPIRA MIRABILIS

Theodore Andrea Cook produced a classic, groundbreaking work, 'The Curves of Life' (1914), exhaustive in its catalogue of myriad spirals and helices in nature, and containing more than 400 illustrations. He came to understand that one of the main beauties of the spiral was that as it was always growing, yet never covering the same ground, it was not simply an explanation of the past but a prophecy of the future. While it defined and illuminated what had already happened, it also led constantly to new discoveries, and he saw that its continuous curve gave the impression of unceasing motion and, in fact, of life itself.

Cook grew up at Wantage after his father Henry was appointed headmaster of King Alfred's School in 1868, a year after his eldest son was born. The boy was strongly influenced by both his parents – his mother Jane was an artist – and he went on to study classics at Oxford, his interest in sport and literature leading him into journalism, a profession in which he gained a high reputation. But his knighthood in 1916 he ascribed modestly more to The Field, of which he had become editor six years before, than to his own merits. The knighthood was in his opinion a recognition of the work for the war effort by the magazine rather than of his own individual contribution.

Having founded the fencing club at Oxford University, Cook became an Olympic swordsman, and it seems apt that a man with the poise of an expert fencer should have written about the elegance of the spiral form. He captained the English Olympic fencing team in 1903 in Paris and again in 1906 in Athens, and the expertise led to his involvement in arrangements for the Olympic Games of 1908 in London. He was one of the three British representatives on the International Olympic Committee. Another great love of his was horseracing and he wrote books and many articles on the subject.

Cook travelled widely in Europe and among the authoritative works he published were 'Old Provence', 'Twenty-five Great Houses of France' and 'Leonardo da Vinci, Sculptor'. He died in 1928, aged 61.

At the beginning of 'The Curves of Life', he states '... for the existence of these chapters upon spiral formations no other apology is needed than the interest and beauty of an investigation which has hitherto only been suggested in a few scattered pamphlets and disconnected references'. He was the first to draw the study of spirals into a comprehensive whole, and his pioneering work deserves much praise. Today, the foundations that he so admirably and painstakingly laid can be used to delve further into the spiral's eternal domain.

Although, after 20 years' involvement with the subject, Cook was ready to suggest that the spiral or helix might lie at the heart of growth, which is life's first principle, and he recorded that it was fundamental to the structure of plants, shells, animals' horns, the human body, even to the periodicity of the atomic elements, it is only to be expected that he was limited by the scientific knowledge and climate of opinion of his day, and could not have imagined the discoveries which lay in the future. Yet he was able to predict, even then, that the story of spirals would be 'the story of the universe'.

Curiously, Edgar Allan Poe's best-selling work in the 1840s was 'The Conchologist's First Book' (1839), a textbook of shells which, needless to say, included many with spiral forms, and in which the introduction pre-echoes Cook, stating: 'The study of conchology . . . will lead the mind of the investigator through paths hitherto but imperfectly trodden to many novel contemplations of Almighty Beneficence and Design.' More than 200 shells were illustrated in this book, which was really a piece of hack writing from which Poe hoped to earn enough to support him until he could make literary connections in Philadelphia. It was actually the work of Professor Thomas Wyatt, a neighbour of Poe's, who had previously published a manual of conchology which was too expensive to reprint, and who thought Poe's name would increase sales and avoid copyright problems.

Interestingly, the photographer for 'The Curves of Life' was Frederick H Evans (1853–1943), dubbed 'the most artistic of photographers' by the playwright George Bernard Shaw. Evans had already collaborated with Cook on his 'Twenty-five Great Houses of France'. The foremost British photographer in the early 1900s, Evans was a bookseller and collector, known and respected by many of the famous artists, writers and critics of the day. At a time when Darwinians suggested an absence of divine meaning in life, Evans believed the world was constructed on intelligible principles and that there was an order to creation. Through his early landscape and nature photography he attempted to show that the physical realm corresponded to the spiritual.

Fascinated by the views he saw under a microscope, he made 'photomicrographs' of minute shells, the eye of a water beetle, and the spine of a sea urchin. In 1887, he received the Photographic Society's Medal of Honour for these artistic studies, and at the age of 45, he sold his bookshop and took up photography full time to pursue a 'life-long study of the beautiful'.

Evans became most famous for his photographs of the great medieval cathedrals of England and France. Always searching for relationships between light and dark, Evans strove to express what he regarded as the 'divine plan' on which these buildings had been founded. His sensitivity to organic forms was always to the fore, and he endeavoured to capture the soul of a cathedral, believing that 'the structural qualities of a Gothic cathedral are very closely allied to those organic principles which underlie the growth or cohesion of living things'.

Obviously, as far as Cook and 'The Curves of Life' was concerned, Evans was the man for the job.

A few years after publication of 'The Curves of Life', D'Arcy Wentworth Thompson, an inspired mathematician, naturalist, Greek scholar and author of 'On Growth and Form' (1917), also examined spirals in nature and came to regard them as providing evidence for a fundamental geometry of creation. The first biomathematician, his dictum was that 'the harmony of the world is made manifest in Form and Number'.

He concluded that the state, including the shape or form, of a piece of matter was the result of a number of forces representing or symbolising the manifestations of various kinds of energy. One is led to believe, he said, that the variety of spiral shells, for instance, 'have grown according to laws so simple, so much in harmony with their material, with their environment, and with all the forces internal and external to which they are exposed, that none is better than another and none fitter or less fit to survive'.

Thompson, a true polymath, wrote about 300 scientific articles and books, but all his aptitudes coalesced in 'On Growth and Form', his most famous work. In it, he assumes that all science and learning are one, and he tries to make biological phenomena conform to mathematics. He was convinced that all animals and plants could be understood only in terms of pure mathematics. He wrote: '... something of the use and beauty of mathematics I think I am able to understand. I know that in the study of material things number, order, and position are the threefold clue to exact knowledge, and that these three, in the mathematician's hands, furnish the first outlines for a sketch of the universe.'

Born in 1860 in Edinburgh, Thompson set out to study medicine at the city's university, but changed to natural sciences at Cambridge and, at the age of 25, he was elected to the chair of biology at the new University College, Dundee. In 1917, he was appointed professor of natural history at the University of St Andrews, where his striking figure was often seen striding through the streets, sporting a wide-brimmed hat and flowing cape. An eccentric character, he would sometimes lecture with a parrot on his shoulder. He was knighted in 1937.

Nautilus pompilius – the shell most closely resembling the curve of the equiangular, or logarithmic, spiral.

Thompson was critical of zoologists of his day for not taking a mathematical approach. He said: 'Even now the zoologist has scarce begun to dream of defining in mathematical language even the simplest organic forms. When he meets with a simple geometrical construction, for instance in the honeycomb, he would fain refer it to psychical instinct, or to skill and ingenuity, rather than to the operation of physical forces or mathematical laws; when he sees in snail, or nautilus, or tiny foraminiferal or radiolarian shell, a close approach to sphere or spiral, he is prone of old habit to believe that after all it is something more than a spiral or a sphere, and that in this 'something more' there lies what neither mathematics nor physics can explain. In short, he is deeply reluctant to compare the living with the dead, or to explain by geometry or by mechanics the things which have their part in the mystery of life.'

Importantly, as Cook and Thompson knew, forms such as the mollusc shells, the horns of rams, goats and so on, even whirlpools, weather systems and the arms of spiral galaxies containing billions of stars, are closely related to the marvellous curve known as the equianglar or logarithmic spiral, the properties of which were first expounded upon by Rene Descartes (1596–1650), the French philosopher and mathematician, and Jacques Bernoulli (1654–1705), the Swiss mathematician, in the 17th century.

In mathematics there are, of course, many different kinds of spiral, the seven most recognised ones being the logarithmic (or equiangular), the Archimedean, the hyperbolic, or reciprocal (the inverse of the

Archimedean), Fermat's, or parabolic, the lituus (the inverse of Fermat's), the square root, and the Golden. As this book does not set out to be a mathematical treatise – such content being outside its intended confines in any event – I shall be discussing primarily the logarithmic spiral, which, with its close relative, the Golden, is the most relevant to my theme, for reasons which will become apparent.

However, I feel it would be worthwhile to give some account of the spiral in the history of mathematics for, on the heels of Descartes and Bernoulli, a whole series of eminent scholars and scientists became attracted to the wonders of it down the centuries, each of their individual contributions making possible today's holistic view of the universe as fundamentally spiral in structure.

The study of spirals probably began with Archimedes (287–212BC), the greatest mathematician of antiquity and, indeed, probably of all time, one of whose books, dating from 225BC, was entitled simply 'On Spirals'. Archimedes was a native of Syracuse, Sicily. His methods anticipated the integral calculus 2,000 years before Newton and Leibniz. It is highly likely that when he was a young man Archimedes studied with the successors of Euclid in Alexandria. Certainly, he was completely familiar with the mathematics developed there, and knew personally the mathematicians of that city.

In 'On Spirals', Archimedes defines the spiral which took his name, and describes its properties. The spiral has turns about the centre which become more and more nearly circular (as in a roll of wallpaper), in contrast to the equiangular spiral whose turns continually increase their width in a constant ratio. It is the first mechanical curve – one traced by a moving point – ever considered by a Greek mathematician. It had already been considered by Archimedes' lifelong friend, the mathematician Conon of Samos (280–220BC), who is said to have served as a kind of court astronomer to Ptolemy III in Alexandria, and with whom Archimedes exchanged mathematical ideas.

This is how Archimedes defines the spiral at the beginning of 'On Spirals': 'If a straight line one extremity of which remains fixed is made to revolve at a uniform rate in a plane until it returns to the position from which it started, and if, at the same time as the straight line is revolving, a point moves at a uniform rate along the straight line, starting from the fixed extremity, the point will describe a spiral in the plane.'

Pappus of Alexandria (c290–350AD), the last of the great Greek geometers, says the spiral of Archimedes was discovered by Conon, although much used by the former. Although Conon was cited as the propounder of a theorem about the spiral in a plane, which Archimedes proved, Pappus' claim is unlikely because Archimedes wrote that he sent certain theorems, without proofs, to Conon. Pappus' major work in geometry, 'Synagoge' or the 'Mathematical Collection', a collection of mathematical writings in eight books thought to have been written in about 340AD (although some historians believe Pappus had completed it by 325AD), includes properties of curves, including the spiral of Archimedes, in its fourth book.

Archimedes was the inventor of the famous 'screw' by which water is raised by the revolution of a pipe twisted in a right-handed helix around a rod, and which is still in use in many parts of the world today, particularly along the River Nile. The screw is also the basis for the present day trommel used in gold mining activities – a rotating sieve or screen which washes and sorts ore. Archimedes built the prototype prospector's spiral separator and studied its ability, with water flowing over it, to elevate minerals in the direct order of their density, just as a panning machine elevates gold and separates it from materials of lesser density.

It should be pointed out that Fermat's and the lituus are both species of Archimedes' spiral. Pierre de Fermat (1601–65), a contemporary of Descartes, was studying analytical geometry at the same time as his eminent compatriot, although Fermat was actually a lawyer and only an amateur mathematician. It was in 1636 that Fermat started investigating the parabolic curve that was to take his name. It is called a dual Fermat's spiral when both its negative and positive values are presented, the central section of it then closely resembling the yin-yang symbol. Practisers of omphaloskepsis – contemplating one's navel as a method of achieving higher meditative levels – adopted this spiral as their symbol.

Roger Cotès (1682–1716), a mathematician and philosopher who was appointed a professor of astronomy at Cambridge at the age of 24, was the first to study the lituus curve and give it its name, a term we have already encountered in the type of divining rod said to have been used by Romulus to lay out the boundaries of Rome. Colin Maclaurin (1698–1746), elected professor of mathematics at Aberdeen at the age of 19, confirmed the name in his book 'Harmonia Mensurarum' (1722), noting the resemblance of the curve to a crozier, a bishop's hooked staff.

The remarkable property of the equiangular spiral, so named by Descartes, is that it is the only mathematical curve which increases by growth at one end but keeps the form of the entire figure, a characteristic which is known as self-similarity. The term 'logarithmic' comes from the way in which the radius of the spiral increases as its curve is described clockwise. The spiral is called 'equiangular' because of another special

51

property – if a straight line is drawn from the central point, or pole, of the spiral to any point on its curve, it always crosses the curve at exactly the same angle. In past times, the pole was known as the 'eye of God'.

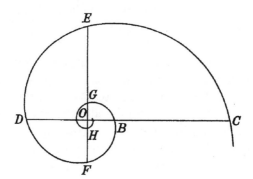

The equiangular, or logarithmic, spiral.

The shell of the chambered nautilus, the tusks of elephants, warthogs and of the extinct mammoths and sabre-tooth tigers, the horn of the rhinoceros, the tooth of the beaver, the claws of cats, beaks of birds and teeth of rodents, all display the same curve. Cook explained how this curve is found in the plant world too, in the successive sprouting of shoots from a stem or branch which also twists into a helicoid shape. The natural forms he noted can be classed together by their incremental, proportional growth in which each successive addition (gnomon) leaves the form of the whole unchanged. Today, this gnomonic aspect of the spiral curve can be viewed fractally – a fractal being a term introduced to mathematics in the 1970s and used to describe a figure in which each part bears the same statistical character as the whole. This idea that a small part of a figure can reflect the totality may also be applied to ourselves, poised between microcosm and macrocosm on a cosmic scale ranging from the sub-molecular world to human existence, to the Earth, the solar system, the galaxy and thence to the universe at large: the Hermetic fractal.

Bernoulli, captivated by the features of the logarithmic spiral, its ability to promote growth while conserving form, was aware of its symbolic potential. Saying that it was representative 'either of fortitude and constancy in adversity, or of the human body which, after all its changes, even after death, will be restored to its exact and perfect self', he seemed to intuit its efficacy in growth and survival throughout nature, and as a model for spiritual advancement.

@ Studies during the NASA Spacelab's first mission in 1983
   confirmed Charles Darwin's theory that some internal,
   biological mechanism guides plant tip growth in an upward
   oscillating spiral. It was found that this growth pattern
   appeared in space, giving the lie to suggestions that gravity
   or other outside forces create the spiralling movement,
   which is known as nutation. On Spacelab, a boxful of dwarf
   sunflowers spiralled without gravity.

New Scientist, April, 1984

The first discussion of the logarithmic spiral appears in letters from
Descartes to Marin Mersenne (1588–1648), the French philosopher and
mathematician, in 1638, which the latter distributed. As a result of this,
the Italian physicist Evangelista Torricelli (1608–47), who invented the
barometer and was secretary and companion to Galileo, worked independently on the spiral's properties, his definition of it being that the radii are
in geometric progression if the angles increase uniformly.

In considering the structure of spiral shells, the English architect
Sir Christopher Wren (1632–1723), who was responsible for the design
of the new St Paul's Cathedral and many of London's churches, and a
contemporary of Bernoulli's, perceived that the spiral was a cone
coiled about an axis.

Edmund Halley (1656–1742), the English astronomer and mathematician, noting that the lengths of the segments of the spiral divided off
from a fixed radius by successive turns of the curve continued in proportion, named it the 'proportional spiral'.

Probably the first to indicate the organic aspects of the logarithmic
spiral was the Scottish mathematician, physicist and inventor Sir John
Leslie (1766–1832) who, in a publication in 1821, 'Geometrical Analysis
and Geometry of Curved Lines', drew attention to its resemblance to
the nautilus shell.

Leslie was steeped in the history of science and the geometry and
philosophy of the Ancient Greeks and, as a teacher, was known to
enthuse over mathematical problems as if they were the most beautiful
examples of classical art, so it is not surprising that he was attracted to
the properties of the logarithmic spiral.

A man of immense knowledge and learning, he applied the abstract
properties of number to a whole range of experimental philosophies, and
was a prolific inventor, inventing the pyroscope, a differential thermo-
meter, a hygrometer and a photometer. For a time, he was private

tutor to the famous Wedgwood family. He published widely, his most notable work being 'An Experimental Inquiry into Heat' (1804).

He was appointed chair of mathematics at Edinburgh in 1805, and five years later, while engaged in experimental research he became interested in heat transfer and was the first to create artificial ice using an air pump. In 1819, he became professor of natural philosophy at Edinburgh (where the Scott monument in East Princes Street Gardens is in the form of a spiral Gothic cross with a central canopy, under which is a statue of Scott with his dog Maida).

Following his proof that the involutes of a logarithmic spiral are themselves logarithmic spirals, he stated: 'The figure thus produced by a succession of coalescent arcs described from a series of interior centres exactly resembles the general form and the elegant septa of the nautilus.'

After Leslie, the Rev H Moseley, a canon at Bristol, made an exacting geometrical examination of turbine shells, reporting in 'On the Geometrical Forms of Turbinated and Discoid Shells' (1838) that the spiral curve around the shell's central axis was indeed logarithmic. This was one of the earliest mathematical discussions of organic logarithmic spirals and it remains one of the classic works of natural history.

The Scottish anatomist and biologist, Professor John Goodsir (1814–67), who was among the first to ask if the equiangular spiral was in fact the manifestation of a law of growth, became so immersed in the subject that he ordered such a spiral to be carved on his gravestone in Edinburgh. The mason, however, failed to do the exacting job properly and after Goodsir's death his family set up a bronze portrait of him instead.

Amazingly, 160 years earlier, the same thing had happened to Bernoulli, who produced a treatise on the logarithmic spiral with the title 'Spira Mirabilis' ('Wonderful Spiral'). Bernoulli was so impressed by the beauty of the shape that, in imitation of Archimedes who had a spiral on his tombstone, he wanted the 'Spira Mirabilis' on his, together with the motto: *Eadem mutato resurgo* – 'although changed, I rise again the same'. But, by mistake, the mason engraved an Archimedian spiral, a blunder that would no doubt have caused Bernoulli much anguish. Clearly, the 'wonderful spiral' has not been so wonderful for the masons of the past!

Goodsir was a member of the Universal Brotherhood of the Friends of Truth, comprising artists, scholars, naturalists and others who became an important influence on the scientific thought of the day. Human anatomy, pathology and morphology was Goodsir's chief sphere of study, and in 1840 he moved to Edinburgh where, in the following year, he was appointed conservator of the Museum of the College of Surgeons. Much of his reputation came to rest on his knowledge of the anatomy of tissues. He is now credited with being the first person to successfully recognise and treat a bacterial infection, ahead of Louis Pasteur.

Goodsir also wrote on morphological subjects, and on the structure of organised forms. He theorised that the triangle was the mathematical figure upon which nature had founded both the organic and inorganic worlds, and he hoped the theory would be his crowning achievement, but he was never to complete this work. To Goodsir, the equiangular spiral stood for the fundamental principle of beauty and growth in nature.

In the mid-19th century, a contemporary of Goodsir's, the embryologist and histologist Martin Barry (1802–55) was involved in a great controversy over a thesis he produced on the microscopic structure of animal and vegetable tissue. Barry asserted that minute double spirals were ubiquitous in the make-up of a wide range of structures, and he set out to convince colleagues of the truth of his claims. Prominent figures, such as Richard Owen and Jan Evangelista Purkyne, agreed that Barry's spirals were real, while others, particularly William Sharpey, were convinced that they were non-existent and that Barry was unreliable as a scientific investigator.

Ultimately, Barry's claims were rejected but, following the discovery of the DNA double helix in the mid-20th century, we can see that he was closer to the truth than he himself probably knew.

After Cook and Thompson, it was not until 1974 that the next popular study of the spiral appeared, although narrower in content and approach. This was 'The Mystic Spiral: Journey of the Soul', by Jill Purce, an artist and lecturer in art, music and mysticism, who produced an appreciation of the spiral as the natural form of growth, and as the symbol of the soul's progress towards eternal life, and also touched on the theme of the labyrinth.

DIVINE PROPORTION

'Geometry has two great treasures. One is the theorem of Pythagoras; the other, the division of a line into extreme and mean ratio. The first we may compare to a measure of gold; the second we may name a precious jewel.'

Johannes Kepler (1571–1630)

The logarithmic spiral's structure is closely related to patterns governed by the Golden Ratio and Divine Proportion rectangles and triangles, the sides of which are in the proportion 1 : 1.618, a figure which possesses some amazing properties. Golden spirals are created by constructing quarter-circles inside the squares of Golden rectangles, which have the special property that when a square is cut off, the remaining shape is another Golden rectangle. A logarithmic spiral can be created from either a Golden rectangle or triangle by geometric methods.

The ratio 1 : 1.618 was integral to the geometry of antiquity and, although it is not known when it was first discovered or put to use, it came to be used as the basis for the construction of sacred buildings, such as temples and chapels, including the dimensions of the Giza Pyramids and the Greek Parthenon. The ratio is in direct proportion to the human frame, the objective being for those entering these buildings to find themselves placed in harmony with the universe. The Ancient Egyptians' term for the Golden Ratio was *neb* (also meaning 'lord', appearing in the names of pharaohs) which, according to David Furlong in 'The Keys to the Temple' (1975), also means 'the spiralling force of the universe', and was one of the sacred names of the Sphinx.

Plato attested to the longevity of the Egyptian canon of sacred geometry by saying that 'the pictures and statues made ten thousand years ago are in no one particular better or worse than what they now make'. In his comments on natural science and cosmology in the 'Timaeus', he regarded the Golden Section to be the most essential of all mathematical relationships and the key to the physics of the cosmos. Euclid (365–300BC), in 'Elements', wrote of dividing a line at the 0.618 point as 'dividing a line in the extreme and mean ratio'. This later gave rise to the use of the term 'mean' as in the Golden Mean.

Shapes arrived at via the Golden Ratio, also-called the Golden Section or Golden Mean, have long been found aesthetically pleasing in Western cultures, reflecting the balance in nature between symmetry and asymmetry, and it remains frequently in use today in art and design. The intersecting lines of a pentagram, for example, divide themselves up into lengths relative to the Golden Ratio.

The term 'golden ratio' seems to have been used first by Leonardo da Vinci in the phrase *sectio aurea*. He used it to fix the fundamental proportions of his painting 'The Last Supper', including the dimensions of the table at which Christ and the disciples sit and the proportions of the walls and windows behind them.

It was the American mathematician Mark Barr who originated the use of the symbol for the Greek letter *phi* to represent the Golden Ratio. He took this from the first Greek letter in the name of Pheidias, or

Phidias, the greatest of the Ancient Greek sculptors who was believed to have used the Golden Section in his designs. There is even a Pheidias spiral, its shape particularly satisfying aesthetically, which can be developed from the logarithmic spiral, and in which, along a radius, the sum of the distances between two successive curves equals the distance to the next curve.

'Despite Phi's seemingly mystical mathematical origins,' Langdon explained, 'the truly mind-boggling aspect of *phi* was its role as a fundamental building block in nature. Plants, animals and even human beings all possessed dimensional properties that adhered with eerie exactitude to the ratio of *phi* to 1 ... 'When the ancients discovered *phi* they were certain they had stumbled across God's building block for the world, and they worshipped Nature because of that ... The mysterious magic inherent in the Divine Proportion was written at the beginning time.'

Dan Brown, *The Da Vinci Code*, 2003

Specifically related to these spirals and to the Golden Section is the Fibonacci series, a mathematical progression introduced to Europe by Leonardo da Pisa (1170–1250), known as Fibonacci. Each part of the curve of the Pheidias spiral, for example, relates to the next in the series of proportion in which the last two integers of a sequence are added together to make the next number, for example: 1, 2, 3, 5, 8, 13, 21, 34, 55, 89, 144 and so on. The ratio of each term to the previous one gradually converges to a limit of about 1.618.

Although born in Italy, Leonardo da Pisa was educated in North Africa where his father Guglielmo Bonaccio – hence, probably, Fibonacci, deriving from 'filius Bonacci', son of Bonacci – held a diplomatic post. Guglielmo represented merchants of the Republic of Pisa who were trading with Bejaia, a port in north-eastern Algeria. The young Leonardo Fibonacci learned mathematics there under the Moors and, travelling widely with his father, he came to understand the various advantages of Hindu–Arabic mathematics – the decimal system – used in different countries along the North African coast. Leonardo, who was one of the first to introduce the decimal system to Europe, writes about his experiences in his book 'Liber abaci' (1202), which also introduces the Fibonacci progression – illustrated by his famously solving a problem to do with the breeding of rabbits!

The Fibonacci sequence is inherent in the proportions of the human figure, of the growing plant where it allows every leaf maximum equal exposure to life-giving sunlight – these arrangements arising from an innate organising property in the genetic material – and even in the arms of spiral nebulae. It is also lodged in those basic principles underlying the world's greatest art and architecture.

This system of proportion has been given the name 'dynamic symmetry' and, long before Leonardo da Pisa came along, it was used by Ancient Egyptian mathematicians, possibly of the first or second dynasty, in surveying, and later in architecture, after which it was taken up by the Greeks. Scholars in India also had an interest in it in connection with rhythmic patterns formed from one and two-beat notes.

Colin Wilson and Rand Flem-Ath point out that Rocky McCollum, in 'The Giza Necropolis Decoded' (1975), noted that he could draw a Fibonacci spiral touching the apex of each of the three pyramids: 'It folds in on itself at a spot south-east of the pyramids... It is Rand's conviction that Thoth's Holy Chamber lies at the centre of this spiral.' Indeed, the Fibonacci series may have been the origin of Ancient Egyptian harmonic design, offering an alignment with natural growth. As the series progresses, so the ratio between successive numbers moves towards the *neb* – 1:1:1618.

It was the French mathematician Edouard Lucas (1842–91) who, centuries after Leonardo da Pisa, dubbed the series 'Fibonacci numbers', although he did not claim it was the creation of Fibonacci. The numbers can be found manifested in the structure of pineapples and pine cones, for example, and in the heads of daisies and sunflowers. In the head of a sunflower, for example, both clockwise and anti-clockwise spirals are formed by the florets, the ratios of one to the other being adjacent Fibonacci numbers. Beautiful effects can be achieved by creating artificial Fibonacci spirals in the artist's studio or with the use of computer programmes.

The spiral or helical leaf arrangement, or phyllotaxis, which corresponds to the progression in plants and trees, occurs so frequently as to be the norm. Leaves are arranged on the stem in a closely coiled spiral, which is known as a generative spiral, and the angle of each successive leaf to the stem's centre is always about 137.5 degrees, known as the Golden Angle, and makes the most efficient use of space. These arrangements are notable in the willow, oak, hawthorn and hazel – all trees which are linked with the spiral in the realms of earth magic – beech, apple, pear, and in the sedges and plantains.

Experiments by physicists in the 1990s suggested that phyllotaxis simply follows the tendency of physical systems to settle into states that

58

minimise energy. The French mathematical physicists Stephane Douady and Yves Couder set out a theory of the dynamics of plant growth and used computer models and laboratory experiments to show that it reflected the Fibonacci pattern. They placed a dish of silicone oil in a vertical magnetic field which was stronger at the edge of the dish than at the centre. Drops of a magnetic fluid, acting like minuscule bar magnets, and put into the centre of the oil, repelled one another and were propelled outwards, creating spirals along which the drops were separated by the Golden Angle.

Cook, suggesting the possibility that there existed a very real connection between the processes of artistic creation vaguely called 'instinctive' and those principles of natural growth and energy which have been accepted as fundamental, gave examples of how the *phi* progression could be applied to proportion, not only in architecture but in anatomy and in certain famous paintings, such as Botticelli's 'Venus' and Turner's 'Ulysses deriding Polyphemus', and in the Great Pyramid, in the relationship between its base and the length of its slope, or apothem; half the length of the base is in the ratio 1:1.618 with the apothem length. For Cook, the *phi* progression hinted at some relationship between the principles of growth and beauty which could cast light on both.

Coincidentally, or perhaps synchronistically, just as Cook was reading the proofs of 'The Curves of Life', a new book, 'Nature's Harmonic Unity: a treatise on its relation to proportional form' (1911), arrived in the post from New York. Written by the landscape painter Samuel Colman (1832–1920) – famous for his paintings of the Grand Canyon in Arizona – with the lawyer and mathematician Clarence Arthur Coan as editor, it dealt broadly with the same issues, although coming at them from a different angle.

While expressing interest in this example of 'the way in which two minds may be attracted by kindred subjects at the same time, without any knowledge of each other's studies', Cook felt his work gave a better explanation of the phenomena which the two authors were investigating. Colman was more concerned with proportional form, while Cook preferred to consider form in relation to growth; Cook saw Colman as dealing with 'morphology apart from physiology, with form separate from function, whereas in my (Cook's) judgement, considerations of function and growth are essential to the right understanding of form and its proportion'.

'Nature's Harmonic Unity' contains more than 300 illustrations by Colman, while Coan provides the mathematical analysis. It moves through a vast array of subjects including geometry, number and form, form evolution, crystallography, botany, conchology, insects, birds, fish, mammals, and even sound, light, heat, gravitation and architecture.

Colman who, as his paintings testify, had a tremendous zest for life and the aesthetic, was also an etcher, collector (being an authority on Chinese art and porcelain) and an interior designer. He became an associate of the National Academy of Design in 1854 and a full academician ten years later. In 1866, he helped to found the American Society of Painters in Watercolours and was its first president, 1866–71, and was an original member of the Society of American Artists.

Colman and Coan went on to produce a second book, 'Proportional Form: Further Studies in the Science of Beauty, being supplemental to those set forth in Nature's Harmonic Unity', in which there were more than 150 illustrations by Colman and, revisiting many of the subjects in the previous work, the pair also discussed spiral formation and the Golden Section.

However, while perceiving 'divine unity of construction in nature', Colman attempted, somewhat dogmatically, to pin down all phenomena of forms in life and art to one simple mathematical expression when really, as Cook understood, there are always deviations, if only slight, the subtleties of which are far more valuable in terms of beauty and interest than having everything conform to a rigid mathematical 'law'. Simple mathematics, Cook asserted, could never express the whole complex truth of natural phenomena.

After all, neither nature nor the artist gets out a slide-rule before imparting their creations, and to proclaim a mathematical statement encompassing phenomena can be hazardous because it will imply a relationship with the phenomena which, in actuality, exists only in the mathematics.

Yet mathematics is still highly effective in explaining nature, and a solution to the puzzle of why it should be so effective lies in what has been termed the 'modified Platonic view'. Some mathematicians and physicists believe that we do not invent mathematics, but discover or observe it; that mathematics would exist in the universe whether or not the human race existed, that maths, like Plato's Forms, is somehow 'out there' in another dimension waiting to resonate in the sensible world.

The claim is that mathematics is the language of the universe, and that galaxies and other objects display logarithmic spiral curves because the laws of physics can be expressed through mathematical equations – such as Einstein's famous $e = mc^2$ – and because the structure of the universe may be regarded as a fractal (a curve or geometrical figure each part of which has the same statistical character as the whole).

So if we were to make contact with extraterrestrial beings on a planet in some far distant star system, and wished to enter into communication with them, we would simply send them the number 1.618 and they would immediately know what we meant by it because they would be subject to the same mathematics that applied throughout the universe. Moreover, on this faraway world, a being could be writing a book (or whatever was the equivalent activity) on the ubiquity of spirals.

Indeed, ELFRAD (Extremely Low Frequency Research And Development), an American self-funded research group founded in 1986, which tracks radiation on Earth, has found an extremely low frequency signal at phi, or 1.618033 Hertz. ELFRAD recognises the frequency as reflecting the Golden Ratio but the signals appear with no clear relationship to any known source. They are not related to solar anomalies or any known weather pattern. They vary in amplitude or intensity and are irregular in timing. ELFRAD continues to monitor the signals, which have been detected on a global scale.

The thinking behind notions of a mathematical universe is not all that new. Four hundred years ago, the German astronomer and mathematician Johannes Kepler said that geometry had 'supplied God with patterns for the creation of the world', and Galileo (1564–1642), the Italian astronomer and physicist, believed that the universe was written in the language of mathematics, without the understanding of which one was lost in a 'dark labyrinth'.

In later centuries, Newton and Laplace concurred with these views, and in the 20th century mathematicians such as G H Hardy and Roger Penrose championed the Platonic standpoint. In 1978, the Russian astronomer Prof K P Butusov announced that he had calculated that the mean planets' cycle times in our solar system concurred with the Golden geometrical progression to a reliability of 95 per cent.

If God is a mathematician, then he is especially fond of the spiral and the Golden Ratio.

'. . . this **Phi** relationship as it manifests in the organic world is intrinsically connected with the growth and development of spirals, helices, of which the most prominent in the whole of nature is, of course, DNA.'

Michael Hayes, *High Priests, Quantum Genes: science, religion and the theory of everything*, 2004

LIFE-SUPPORTING, LIFE-PROTECTING

The 'magneto-protective' qualities of spirality – recall the young girl's spiral mandala referred to by Jung – together with the aspects of fertility as disclosed by Herbert Weaver, may perhaps be applied in combination to the life-supporting structures of galaxies and to the molecular architecture of the genetic material in the DNA helix. Evidence for the acknowledgement of the efficacy of the spiral form is found throughout nature and the animal kingdom.

Eddies in moving water have a special 'within-ness' which is different from the 'without-ness' of the stream. It is also interesting that eddies and spirals, whether in water, air, weather systems, or in animal tissue in the form of tusks and horns, often tend to come in 'mirror image' pairs – just dip your hand in a bowl of water to see these twin vortices form.

It has been suggested that fish propel themselves forward by generating their own eddies, and that flocks of birds fly in 'V' formations to gain lift from each other's aerial eddies and wakes. The movement of a bird's wing-tip in flight, moreover, describes a line of which each section is part of a spiral. The peregrine falcon swoops on its prey in a logarithmic spiral trajectory, on the axiom that the straight line drawn from the pole (in this case, the prey) to any point on its curve always crosses the curve at exactly the same angle.

Dowser Guy Underwood found that, in the open, animals and birds choose to give birth to their young above 'blind springs', where water comes almost to the surface, and which he saw as the nodal points of geodetic lines of influence in the earth, these lines converging on the nodes in spirals which often took seven turns about the centre. Underwood concluded that such places had a health-giving or restorative property which was instinctively sought out by the animal kingdom. There was some indication, he felt, that the spirals found at the locations of blind springs either eased labour or produced healthier offspring, or both.

Retired from the legal profession, Underwood (1883–1964) taught himself water divining and became a pioneer in the field of what has become earth energy dowsing. His geodetic system traces naturally occurring patterns and 'lines of influence' in the landscape which can be discovered by dowsing especially, but not exclusively, at ancient tracks and sacred sites. Some of these lines and patterns are related to underground watercourses. Underwood maintained that ancient sites and trackways were deliberately located so as to coincide with these features – hence the title of his book 'The Pattern of the Past' (1969), published widely only posthumously, with the assistance of John

Michell. Geodetics may be seen as a genuine attempt to understand the efficacy of the divining rod, and to relate the natural energies to which it responds to the behaviour of plants, animals and people.

According to Underwood, geodetic lines usually take winding courses and may be zig-zag, looped or folded into hair-pin curves, often keeping to one general direction for some distances. Multiple lines have religious significance, their presence frequently indicated at stone circles and other megalithic sites by notches or grooves on the stones. Sites such as Stonehenge or the Bradbury Circle at Bradford-on-Avon, he found, have loops and spirals formed by these 'primary lines' which converge on and emanate from blind springs where the effect is to cause the converging lines to turn into spirals. These 'primary spirals', as he called them, enclose the spring and centre on it.

@ **'The broader significance of the Earth Force must lie in its effect upon animal and vegetable life. The philosophers and priests of the old religions seem to have believed that – particularly when manifested in spiral forms – it was involved not only as a catalyst with the construction of matter but also with the generative powers of nature; that it was part of the mechanism by which what we call Life comes into being; and to have been the 'Great Arranger' – that balancing principle which keeps all Nature in equilibrium, and for which biologists still seek.'**

Guy Underwood, *The Patterns of the Past*, 1969

A nest chamber internally protected with a spiral form and externally marked with serpentine ridges is made by the oven bird of South America, and the egg-purses of the Port Jackson and other sharks are of spiral design, as are the arrangement of their teeth and intestines. Mexican free-tailed bats swarm from their caves in their thousands in a left-handed helix pattern.

The case made by the larvae of the caddis fly is of a spiral shape, the spider spins her web with a spiral movement, and just as certain shells have a strengthening spiral coil around their central columns, so do insects and plants have a spiral thickening in the walls of their tracheas, or air-tubes. Animals such as the ram rely on the spiral and curved forms in their horns. The gills of the tube-building worm *sabella* are set in a spiral, presumably to create a vortex in water to suck food towards the mouth.

Both univalve and bivalve molluscs have shells of voluted structure, shielding the breathing organs and heart, and the animal itself from injury or attack. Among the molluscs, which form the world's largest body of animals after the insects, are the *helicidae*, a major family of land gastropods which includes the common snail, and the *volutidae*, their marine counterparts, including the well-known nautilus, in whose shells the spiral form attains perfection.

The fragile shell of the female paper nautilus, *argonauta argo*, protects her growing embryos, of which there may be as many as 50,000 at any one time. Only the female secretes the thin shell that gives the species its name. The paper nautilus is a cephalopod, which is a type of mollusc related to the octopus and squid, and lives in warm, tropical seas.

The tropical marine gastropod *turritella*, or screw shell, has a long, distinctive spiral shell composed of whorls around a central rigid spine, called the columella. As the animal grows in the end whorl, it continues to secrete calcium carbonate along the outer rim, causing the shell to grow longer over time. Another marine gastropod, *tonna galea*, or tun, has a complex coiled shell of spiral form which saves the creature – in this case a carnivore which paralyses and kills its prey by injecting it with acid through its jaw plates – from building a long shell which could slow its movement.

Many varieties of foraminifera, the smallest animals, have chalky shells in logarithmic spiral forms which have remained virtually unchanged for millions of years. These creatures are so abundant that their shelly remains, as chalk, make up a major part of a number of sedimentary limestones. The protozoan Vorticella (from the Latin for 'vortex') have spiral cilia, possibly to draw in food. And probing deeper into the microscopic world of nature, one finds that many types of bacteria, such as the spirillum, and the spermatazoa of all higher animals, have helical structures. Spirogyra, a genus of freshwater algae, has chlorophyll in spiral bands, while volutella is a genus of imperfect fungi which causes dry-rot in plants.

A strange helical fossil, known as the Devil's Corkscrew, is found in great numbers in parts of Nebraska and Wyoming in the USA. They are giant quartz spirals, more than six feet tall, and their origin is attributed to the ancestors of modern beavers which made helical burrows, similar but smaller fossils being found in Europe. Spiralities can also be observed in fossil ammonites and scaphites which can reach the enormous size of two feet in diameter.

The propulsive force afforded by the screw or spiral is made use of in nature in scores of impressive ways: the heart of man and of most other

64

mammals is made in this way, fibres in the ventricles running in spiral lines from the tip of the base of this vital organ so that the muscular constriction by which the blood is forced onward, and the circulation kept up, is like the twist of a screw.

Medical scientists working with aeronautical engineers at Imperial College, London, reported that nature has designed human arteries with a helical twist to encourage a swirling blood flow which might well prevent the arteries 'furring up'. The discovery may change the way surgeons perform heart operations, in that new and better bypass grafting techniques, which take account of blood swirling, can be developed. Professor Colin Caro said: 'A helical pipe is a much better model for blood in arteries than a two-dimensional structure.'

Press Association, London, May 1998

The human umbilical cord is a wonderful example of a (left-handed) triple helix of two veins and an artery, and the power of many of the bones in our bodies – the humerus and the pelvis, for instance – is derived from a similar form.

Although the less complex relative of the spiral, the helix is also fundamental to living things. While the spiral curve moves steadily away from a point of origin, the helix simply twists along within the same diameter, this being the reason for its importance, the difference between a spiral and a helix being that of a helter skelter slide and the rifling in a gun barrel. The helix concentrates the lateral energy of the spiral and makes it vertical, giving it, in the words of Horace Freeland Judson, 'an aggressive, penetrating structure, well-designed to accomplish special, urgent tasks', as exemplified in drill bits and the usually misnamed 'spiral' staircase, the actual helical structure of which makes for highly efficient use of living space.

'Look for patterns of growth and you find helices. Their elegant and economical forms are the solutions to innumerable puzzles of how to plan and build animals and plants.' The helix is a curve nature 'finds seductive'.

Dr John Galloway, a writer on molecular biology, discussing the asymmetry of helices. *New Scientist*, January 1983

Anatomically, the helix is the name given to the rim of the human ear which parallels the profile of the curled-up human foetus head down in the womb, in itself reminiscent of the spiral or 'S' shape (the contour of the human embryo follows the curve of the logarithmic spiral). In the 'labyrinth' of the inner ear, and coiled in the shape of a snail shell, is to be found the cochlea, a division of the ear which analyses frequencies and is well-developed in mammals and birds – in humans consisting of a spiral canal in which lies a smaller membranous spiral passage.

The word 'cochlea' comes from the Latin for snail shell, Archimedean screw, or a spiral stairway, and from the Greek word denoting the snail and also those kinds of shellfish with spiral shells.

The cochlea contains the organ of Corti (named after Alfonso Corti, 1822–76, the Italian anatomist) which in mammals is the main if not the only part of the ear by which sound is directly perceived. It contains two spiral rows of minute 'rods of Corti' which arch over a spiral 'tunnel of Corti' and support hair cells connected to the spiral ganglion of the cochlear nerve itself. The 'labyrinthine sense' is the name given to that complex sense concerned with the perception of bodily position and motion, mediated by organs in the ear and stimulated by the pull of gravity and movements of the head.

Biophysicists and biochemists have investigated spiral patterns which are created by certain chemical reactions. These patterns are formed by a spiral wave which the reactions self-organise in space and time. American biophysicist Arthur Winfree discovered how two factors collaborate to generate these spirals (the appearance of which is akin to the Archimedean variety) each of which factor by itself would result only in a homogenous steady state.

One is the purely physical process of molecular diffusion, and the other is the purely chemical process of reaction. 'In combination, the two give rise to an activity that is almost lifelike,' he said ('Scientific American', June, 1974). Winfree's work followed that of the Russian scientists Zhabotinsky and Zaikin who, in the 1960s, had encountered such spirals in a reagent they produced from a mixture of bromine compounds, malonic acid and the indicator dye, iron phenanthroline.

This 'Z' reagent, as Winfree dubbed it, is mostly red in colour, due to the bromine, and blue waves of chemical activity are propagated through it at a rate of several millimetres a minute, inducing the spiral patterns. In fact, Russian biophysicists and mathematicians, in attempting to understand flutter and fibrillation in the heart, were studying spiral waves years before the chemical phenomenon was discovered, in the context of electrically excited waves circulating around obstacles in heart muscle.

Weather patterns also take spiral forms, as exemplified in awesome tropical typhoons and hurricanes, and in whirlwinds or waterspouts where columns of air spiral violently upwards. Tropical cyclones form when moist air over the sea is forced to rise. As the air rises, it expands and cools, creating spiralling cloud formations which are visible from space. The eye of the storm is formed as dry air from above sweeps into the low pressure area at the centre and plummets downwards, leaving a circular area free of cloud surrounded by a cylindrical wall of thunder clouds.

The spirality of these storm clouds is caused by the 'Coriolis effect', a consequence of the rotation of the Earth. In the northern hemisphere the spiral turns anti-clockwise, and in the southern hemisphere, clockwise.

Spiral hurricane formation.

Cloud systems of hurricanes can be twice the height of Mount Everest. The 2004 Roland Emmerich disaster movie, 'The Day After Tomorrow', about sudden climate shift due to global warming, abounds with dramatic portrayals of spiralling storms seen from space and in computer simulations.

Spiral formations are also to be found in the atmospheric phenomenon known as Von Karman vortices. These constitute a long string of eddies which rotate alternately clockwise and anti-clockwise, and which are caused by obstacles, such as islands, which disturb the air flow as it passes. These vortices are frequently observed in satellite images of cloud layers over islands, the clouds following the spiral patterns of the eddies.

Weather on Mars has made it the only planet in the solar system where huge ice spirals – following the pattern of the logarithmic spiral – occur at the poles. Just how they came to be created had baffled scientists for decades. But in 2004, it was explained that the spiralling gorges, more than half a mile deep and spread over hundreds of miles, are cut into the ice caps as a result of the particular angle of the planet's tilt, its cold climate and its thin atmosphere.

John Pelletier, a professor of geophysical sciences at the University of Arizona, applied mathematical formulas devolved from spiral patterns formed by slime moulds to simulate the spiral ice canyons. His computer model generated patterns that matched the appearance of the Martian spirals, even including their imperfections.

On Mars, surface temperature is determined strongly by the planet's angle to the Sun, as there is scant movement of heat in the thin atmosphere. Professor Pelletier said that the tilt of the planet caused ice on one side of a crack to heat up and vaporise, enlarging it, both in depth and width. Then the water vapour struck the shady, colder side of the gorge and refroze. The troughs formed through an instability where areas of ice steeper towards the Sun started to melt while other areas stayed frozen. The steep areas got steeper, as they faced even more directly towards the Sun, leading to further melting and a continuation of the melt/freeze process.

Professor Pelletier felt that the logarithmic pattern occurred because the troughs migrated at a slower rate near the poles, because it was colder, resulting in slower melting and a 'bunching' effect. Such ice spirals do not occur at the Earth's polar caps, partly because temperatures are regulated to a degree by global air and ocean currents.

The implication of all the above is that the spiral form is integral to strength and growth and indeed, it may be that all curves of growth are based on it. Moreover, the spiral is a powerful example of how nature tends to repeat the use of a successful design over and over again on every level of its creative handiwork (more on this in chapter six): indeed, the spiral and helical designs are the most universal of all.

The American architect Peter Stevens, in *Patterns in Nature* (1974), describes the spiral as a 'prototypical model of spatial enclosure' which, in wrapping around on itself, creates a sheltered and protective environment.

4

Dragon Magic

'If the spiral is the most widespread prehistoric symbol, perhaps the most universal legend is that of the power of the serpent dragon...'

Francis Hitching, *Earth Magic*, 1976

Mankind has always sought a dialogue with the forces of creation, the symbol of which is the spiral, and, if I may start this chapter on a personal note, I realise now that I was one who sensed 'dragon magic' in the world around me from a very early age, and I am sure many others have too, although, like me, they did not realise what it was at the time.

Even as a small child I was attracted to, and moved by, both sites of antiquity, particularly ancient earthworks, stone circles and standing stones – places where the earth forces were concentrated – and the patterns which the stars made in the night sky. On holiday with my parents in various parts of the country during those years, I always somehow managed to seek out these mysterious, out-of-the-way places which gave wing to my imagination.

I have vivid memories, for example, of the massive earth ramparts of Maiden Castle, that wonder of prehistoric land sculpturing near Dorchester in Dorset, and of crouching excitedly under Cornish quoits and standing stones, where mournful winds seemed to be full of ancient voices and whispered secrets. In dream symbolism, megaliths are often seen as representing the forces of the spirit emerging out of the unconscious, or out of the affairs of life. For me, the old stones stand there as a reminder – to jog our collective memory, as it were – of something important the human race has lost, or at least forgotten, but may yet find again.

John Michell, that dedicated researcher into ancient wisdom, put it well. Such places, he said, 'still bear the invisible marks of some feat of natural magic, performed by the adepts of the former world, space and time travellers, masters of revelation, to whom the earth was but

70

another living creature, responding like man to certain shapes, sounds and poetic correspondences, the keys to universal enlightenment'.

By the age of 11, something equally compelling about the night skies was leading me to compile my own detailed star maps, constellation by constellation, until I was well-versed in the basics of astronomy. Something in me, even then, seemed to intuit that there were connections between the majestic movements of the stars and those old, windswept monuments I loved to visit. During moments of distractedness or preoccupation, at school or at home, I would doodle on notepaper three recurring patterns – a double, or 'mirror-image', spiral, a diamond (or perhaps an octahedron), and a zigzag lightning bolt – without, at the time, realising the significance of them in terms of the collective unconscious.

As the significance of the lightning bolt may not be so readily apparent, I refer again to Jung who said that lightning could signify a 'sudden, unexpected and overpowering change of psychic condition', or at least intuition. The liberating flash of lightning was a symbol used by the Druids, for whom it stood for divine power, and by Paracelsus and the alchemists. We have already seen how zigzag patterns adorn neolithic monuments.

The 'fireflash', or 'sky serpent', was seen by adepts as the originator of life and light, and the medium of a transformative power. It was also frequently depicted as a fiery serpent. Chapter 17 of Luke, in the New Testament, says: 'For as the lightning, that lighteneth out of the one part under heaven, shineth unto the other part under heaven, so shall also the Son of Man be in his day.' And in chapter nine of Zechariah, in the Old Testament, is found: 'And the Lord... his arrow shall go forth as the lightning.'

In the Golden Dawn magical tradition, the idea was to follow the 'zigzag lightning flash' of sacred manifestation as it traced the path of the divine energy of creation through the various sephirah of the Kabbalah's Tree of Life. In Kabbalistic cosmology, the lightning bolt symbolises the universal life force, the divine light having pulsed through the ten levels of increasing intensity before earthing itself in matter. Scientists now believe that it may well have been an electrical emission from a lightning strike which, in the early history of the Earth, brought about the molecular conditions suitable for the building blocks of living matter to be formed.

In Bob Dylan's *Black Diamond Bay*, 1975, the spiral, diamond and fireflash are all present – in images of a spiral staircase, the 'diamond' bay of the title, and a bolt of lightning. And

71

Dylan, with his involuted songs of refuge and resurgence, chose a stage-name which, from the old Druid Welsh, means 'son of the sea wave', itself a link with the volute and the spiral form in nature.

Intuition, certainly, comes to play a major part in any appreciation of earth magic, especially in the location and study of leys, which are the usually ancient alignments in straight lines of hallowed places where earth energies are found to accumulate, the object of these alignments across miles of countryside believed to have been to direct and channel the life-enhancing properties of subtle, regenerative vibrations.

Such places were holy ground, esoteric centres where, according to Guy Underwood, the blind spring designated the centre of the sacred site while its spiral of energy bestowed that 'divine protective sanctity' postulated by students of the old religion. T C Lethbridge (1901–71), the archaeologist, dowser and investigator of the paranormal who studied pagan and Dark Age sites, also referred to force-fields in spiral and conical patterns, and the charging of sacred places with energy – 'from a three-dimensional world I seem to have fallen through into one where there are more dimensions', he famously said. Ancient monuments and many old churches are where they are for very good reasons, their sites not having been decided merely by whim, or aligned simply by chance.

It reminds one of the Don Juan stories of Carlos Castenada in which the old Indian sorcerer chooses special 'power places' – high hills, rocks, ravines, or just on open ground – for magical purposes, or simply as correct spots on which to sit. Similarly, in ancient times, people all over the world knew how to divine the locations of these centres of energy, and they founded their temples on them.

It seems that the standing stones (and later churches and cathedrals) were built on these sites as tuned instruments to amplify and transmit these energies for the benefit of their surrounding communities, a kind of 'earth acupuncture' as Tom Graves put it, symbolised by St Michael, the Christianised guardian of leys, whose pagan equivalent was Hermes, depicted as piercing the coils of a dragon with his lance.

Probably the most famous ley is the St Michael Line, discovered by John Michell, geographically the longest line that can be drawn over land across southern England, running from a point near Land's End in the far south-west to the coast of East Anglia. All along, or close to, its straight path are to be found, by significant coincidence, St Michael sanctuaries including Glastonbury Tor, Burrowbridge, Brentor, Roche Rock, St

Earth energies spiral up through ancient megalithic sites and Christian places of worship sometimes built over them.

Michael's Mount, Carn Brea, as well as the main southern entrance of Avebury Circle.

In their book, 'The Sun and the Serpent' (1989), Paul Broadhurst and the Scottish dowser Hamish Miller detected strange energies which wound around the St Michael Line in a serpentine manner. They were able to trace two lines of current, from Land's End as far as Avebury, which spiralled about the line to form a symbol of the caduceus, which, as we have noted, is the serpent–entwined wand of Hermes.

Michell regards the line as the 'backbone' of southern England, ener-gized by the vital earth currents. The sanctuaries on its course where the two currents meet, such as Glastonbury and Avebury, he says, can be seen as the *chakra* or nodal points in the 'subtle body' of the landscape, its field of geomagnetic and other energies.

Crispin Paine, a heritage consultant whose particular interest is the material culture of religion – how it is expressed in daily life – usefully identifies six types of sacred place: those to which spiritual meaning is attributed, places of memory and myth, places of immanent energy, those created to convey spiritual feelings, or formally set apart by an institution, and places made holy by the presence of a sacred object. Clearly, the first three types can be applied to the kinds of sites mentioned above, and the next two types to the kinds of structures built on them.

By its very nature, a sacred place must be distinct from everywhere else, in some way set apart, and 'guarded by physical, ritual and psychological barriers'. But more than this, sacred places have a use, or they would not continue to exist. They provide a range of benefits and functions held in high regard by the communities that revere them.

The religious scholar Mircea Eliade, famous for his erudite 'Shamanism' (1964), regarded the sacred place as a location where the veil separating the realm of the gods, of grace and the transcendent, from the world of nature and humanity, becomes tenuous, and where a crossing point is made possible between Heaven and Earth. Shamanic methods of attaining ecstasy and passing over this crossing point, of passing through this 'crack between the worlds' – often visualising a spiral as a state of trance is entered – are much the same in tribal cultures everywhere (see Appendix 1).

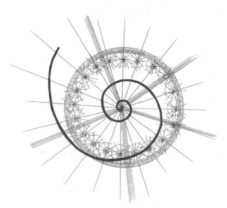

Dowsed energy lines at the Merry Maidens stone circle near Penzance in Cornwall.

Megalithic cultures, as typified by the great stone monuments of Stonehenge and Avebury in England and the Pyramids in Egypt, thrived in a period which corresponded to the Platonic Year of Taurus,

the prevalent characteristics of which made possible the raising of structures which would stand for thousands of years as testimony to the drive
in the people of those times to give their philosophy tangible and, if
possible, everlasting expression. For Taurus, which is an earth sign, is
associated with perseverance, steadfastness, stability and conservation,
while Scorpio, its combining polar opposite, is associated with death,
rebirth and occult power, leading to the links between the impressive
monuments of the epoch and the beliefs then held of an afterlife.

My own interest in earth magic and geomancy, which later led
me to ecology and Jung, was born during a visit in the summer of
1968 to the 12th century 'serpent church' at Kilpeck in Herefordshire.
The effect on the emotions of this magical and peaceful place, with its
castle mound (at least as ancient) nearby, was considerable. An alignment
to Coles Tump on the southern skyline was immediately apparent, and
this became one of the many previously unrecorded leys which I found
in Herefordshire and Worcestershire after I moved to live in that
region in the mid-1970s.

Kilpeck Church is simply festooned with dragons and serpents –
evidence of the old homage that must have been paid to the earth spirit
at this site in past times. Its raised position, and its oval shape, suggest
that it may overlay megalithic remains, and dowsing has shown that
the church – its apse, chancel and nave – is aligned to an underground
stream, the course of which is also followed by the lane which approaches
from the east. This must be why the church is angled slightly away from a
precise east–west orientation.

One of the first things one notices about the exterior decoration of
the church are the corbels at the western end which the guidebook
describes as representing a crocodile swallowing its arch-enemy, the
hydrus, but which can be seen just as surely as dragon heads with spiral
tongues.

The impressively-sculpted main entrance doorway depicts the Tree
of Knowledge of Good and Evil on the tympanum and, on columns
either side, entwined serpents, and the uroborus in an arch above. The
left-hand column also shows two figures, one carrying a lance and the
other a sword, and each wearing a Phrygian cap, a symbol pointing to
the possible survival, or at least memories, of the Mithraic cult in the
area long after the downfall of the Romans who brought it to this
country.

Indeed, many other carvings around the church, including vine
sprigs, and lion and bull heads, suggest a connection between the
site and Mithraism, a link which was still strong perhaps even up to

The ornate main entrance doorway at the 12th century Kilpeck Church in Herefordshire

the time the church was built. In all, there are 85 corbels, a mixture of pagan and Christian symbolism embracing Celtic, Anglo-Saxon, Scandinavian and French Romanesque forms, and including the infamous Sheela-na-gig.

Mithraism was Persian in origin, being based on that people's sun-god Mazda who fought a constant battle against the powers of darkness and evil, and the Roman legions spread it throughout the empire. The red phrygian cap is also a form of headwear associated with Cybele, the earth mother goddess of antiquity and an embodiment of nature and the cosmos, and also, at one time, a goddess of Rome. Cybele is sometimes depicted on a chariot next to the Tree of Life which is entwined by a serpent. This ties in with a depiction of the Green Man, the worldwide symbol of the union of man with the green world of nature, at the top of the column to the right of the church doorway. The west window, surrounded by an intricate interlacing of serpents, and with a pair of Green Men facing one another in profile, is placed high up in the wall, perhaps to allow the sun to shine straight into the apse at certain significant times of the year.

Kilpeck is a prime example of a site which, as a prominent nodal ley centre and focal point of earth energies, already had been considered sacred for thousands of years before the church was built, and whose power was profusely acknowledged, consciously or unconsciously, in the very fabric of the church and the decor its builders came to choose.

It is the kind of story, however, which is repeated in many places around Britain, and also around the world, if only we cared to take notice of the ritualistic signs and messages which our ancestors left for us in the geometry and ornamentation of their monuments, and in the land itself. Early man believed that the earth was inhabited by a spirit, that the earth was not simply inanimate matter but possessed a life and soul of its own. In many cultures this idea came to be identified with an earth goddess, or earth mother, a provider and protector.

It was natural to assume the spirit was female and would give sustenance and 'shelter from the storm' to those who respected her, and Cybele, Ceres, Demeter, Gaia, Ceridwen, Dana, Coatlicul and Kali were some of the names given to her in different parts of the world, all of these figures possibly deriving from Isis of Ancient Egypt, the archetypal Universal Mother. These figures represented fecundity and fruitfulness, cereal, grain, food production and the harvest, nurturing and maternal love. All animate organisms were given life which was returned to the earth at death, in due course to be passed on to other beings. As Nicholas Mann reminds us, this goddess was represented in the archetypal realm by symbols including the spiral, stone, throne, cup and cauldron.

Our ancestors understood life currents to pulse through the earth, sometimes concentrating themselves at certain points which, because it was here that vital energies could be tapped, became holy or at least venerated places. It followed that the priests and wise men of the world, who became sensitive to these invisible earth forces, would devise an arcane system for their acknowledgement by the initiated.

A cosmic code was evolved in antiquity which today we are beginning to crack, although it has lain under our noses, or rather, under our feet, for centuries, and can be traced back to origins in the idea of the Universal Mother.

@ Erich Neumann (1905–60), a student of Jung's, in his *Origins and History of Consciousness*, 1949, takes the uroborus, the snake or 'primal dragon' biting its tail, as the original symbol of the Great Mother. He points to the uroborus also as symbolising the creative impulse of new beginning, the 'wheel that rolls of itself' – 'the initial, rotary movement in the upward spiral of evolution'.

To take account of, channel and enhance the natural energies, earthworks, stone circles and standing stones were erected; naturally occurring features, such as mounds, banks, springs and caves with special qualities endowed by the earth currents, were sought out; and public buildings, roads, walls, bridges and ponds were accordingly positioned. These currents have been called 'geodetic', in the belief that they may be created by variations in terrestrial gravity and magnetism, or simply 'telluric', with the idea that they emanate from the movement of subterranean waters, or magma, or arise from faults in the earth which have brought into contact different soils which, with changes in temperature, generate variations in potential.

As must be fairly well known nowadays, it was, in England, Alfred Watkins, a Hereford antiquarian and visionary with suppressed psychic abilities, who in the early years of the last century rediscovered the ley system, and John Michell who, in the 1960s, suggested that Britain contained only part of what was once a worldwide network of natural magic.

Watkins (1855–1935), who spent the last 14 years of his life gathering evidence to support his controversial ideas, made his momentous discovery on June 30, 1921, when, while on a visit to Blackwardine, near Leominster, he paused to study the map for interesting features. It suddenly dawned on him that a series of straight lines could link all the various landmarks in a network of ancient tracks.

Also a pioneer in photography, Watkins began with a primitive pinhole camera which he made from a cigar box, and went on to devise an exposure meter after working out the mathematical properties of light, the size of the camera lens, and the amount of exposure. He also invented a flour which would make a perfect brown bread, the Vagos or 'Wandering Maiden', from the Roman name for the River Wye, and the loaf soon became popular in his home city. Watkins' association with archaeology led to him joining the Woolhope Naturalists' Field Club, founded in 1851, which was based in Hereford, and he became a leading member of the club, giving many lectures which he illustrated with his own slides.

Michell, born 1933, has become a world authority on ancient science and religion and the symbolism of ancient landscapes. Educated at Eton and Cambridge, his 'The View over Atlantis' (1969) and 'City of Revelation' (1972) played a major part in altering the outlook of a whole generation by revealing the science, culture, spirituality and wisdom of ancient civilisations. Soundly based upon Pythagorean and Platonic ideals, Michell's works combine common sense with a deep understanding of his subject matter, and from the outset he recognised the numerical codes underlying ancient and classical cultures. Whatever their geographical location, the structure of the sacred buildings of these civilisations was founded on the selfsame numerical system.

A detailed exposition of the achievements of these two important figures is unnecessary here and, in any event, students of 'ley power' will be conversant with their writings, which speak best for themselves. It is no coincidence, however, that the evidence for leys within the practice of earth magic around the world is so often found to be linked, sometimes consciously, sometimes unconsciously, with spirality as the premier symbol of its potentialities.

A small example is that Watkins showed that 'dodman', the name given to the early surveyor/geomancer who used a pair of sighting staves to confirm the alignments of leys, was also an old nickname for the snail with its two 'staves' on its head – and, of course, its spiral shell. On a larger scale, among the ancient patterns drawn on the desert plains of Nazca in southern Peru, which include many long, straight tracks, is to be seen one large spiral, and spirals attached to other designs.

One of the most astonishing discoveries of recent years has been that of Tom Brooks, a retired businessman from Devon who, in tribute to Watkins, has spent a lifetime exploring and researching sites of antiquity in southern Britain. After scores of painstaking measurements made over many years, he has found not only that the alignments of ancient sites are founded on the bases of isosceles triangles – ones which have two sides of equal length – but that networks of alignments form great spiral patterns (both right- and left-turning) in the landscape, the spiral 'arms' being produced as a series of interconnected cords which are, in actuality, the bases of adjoining triangles.

The geometry is so sophisticated that, within what seems to be an ever-expanding system under which all points in a landscape can be contacted in a predetermined manner, Brooks is able to predict the next step between units – the next link in the chain – before actually arriving at the proof.

I shall dwell on Brooks' work at some length because I believe it to be of profound significance. If the purpose of the alignments of ancient sites was navigational, as he suggests, then spirality was clearly integral to this early form of mapping.

One vast system consists of a clockwise and an anti-clockwise spiral centred on Silbury Hill in Wiltshire, which he regards as 'the prime generator in pre-history of an expanding web of communication that reached all parts of Britain (and beyond) in a pre-planned, mathematically sound and integrated manner'. The system unravels outwards until it reaches the coasts. A similar system, embracing the sites of churches, abbeys, priories and cathedrals, is centred on Wells Cathedral in Somerset, suggesting that the plan for the location of Christian houses in England was based on the prehistoric model of at least 3,000 years before.

Brooks offers proof that ancient British surveyors constructed a geodetic network linking hill settlements with barrows by stone and mound markers, each related geometrically to a central node, these align-ments of prehistoric sites, radiating in spiral patterns, allowing ancient peoples to find their way safely and reliably about the country. Geometry based on what already existed would have positioned the hub of the 'navigational wheel' at a particular spot, and if there was no high ground available, it would have had to be created.

Thus Silbury Hill – dating from about 3000BC – became 'the epitome of Stone Age mesolithic industry'. It is so large, not because it was the burial place of a chieftain, as has been the conventional view, but because of the required lines of sight to many other surrounding sites, especially Marlborough Mound, five and a half miles distant.

Silbury Hill's huge size, with its finished surface of interlocked chalk blocks, was needed also to reflect its importance in the system of geometry that flowed from it, and to command respect from all who encountered it. All archaeological research surrounding Silbury Hill has been based on the premise that the prehistoric inhabitants were primitive, even barbaric, and concerned more with death, burial and ritual worship rather than being intelligent and cultured, says Brooks.

Current and past thinking is mistaken in regarding hillforts as the randomly arranged, unrelated defensive positions of warring factions, and barrows and mounds as having been constructed for the sole purpose of ritual burial. Brooks argues that: hillforts were not the defen-sive positions of warring tribes but neighbourly settlements designed to keep out wild animals; long barrows were not places of ritual burial but a kind of neolithic 'motel' where travellers on the 'straight tracks' would shelter while passing between settlements; and the small so-

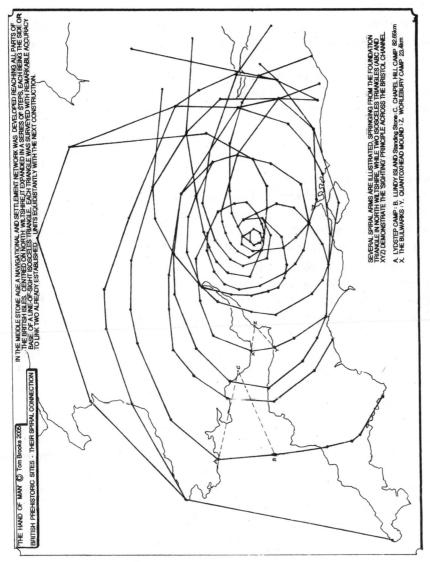

THE HAND OF MAN © Tom Brooks 2009

BRITISH PREHISTORIC SITES - THEIR SPIRAL CONNECTION

IN THE MIDDLE STONE AGE A NAVIGATIONAL AND SETTLEMENT NETWORK WAS DEVELOPED REACHING ALL PARTS OF THE BRITISH ISLES. CENTRED ON NORTH WILTSHIRE, IT EXPANDED IN A SERIES OF STEPS, EACH BEING THE SIDE OR BASE OF A LINE-OF-SIGHT ISOSCELES TRIANGLE. EACH TRIANGLE WAS SURVEYED WITH REMARKABLE ACCURACY TO LINK TWO ALREADY ESTABLISHED UNITS EQUIDISTANTLY WITH THE NEXT CONSTRUCTION.

SEVERAL SPIRAL ARMS ARE ILLUSTRATED, SPRINGING FROM THE FOUNDATION TRIANGLE IN NORTH WILTSHIRE, WHILE TWO ISOSCELES TRIANGLES (ABC AND XYZ) DEMONSTRATE THE SIGHTING PRINCIPLE ACROSS THE BRISTOL CHANNEL.

A. LYDSTEP CAMP : B. LUNDY ISLAND Standing Stone : C. CHAPEL HILL CAMP 82.66km
X. THE BULLWARKS : Y. QUANTOXHEAD MOUND : Z. WORLEBURY CAMP 23.4km

Tom Brooks' discovery of a spiral system of alignments of ancient sites throughout southern England and Wales.

called burial mounds, or tumuli, and standing stones were 'signposts' or markers on the tracks.

As Ancient Britons pondered how best to explore the wild country-side around them, following the last Ice Age, they would have been faced with water levels much higher than today due to melting ice. Estimating conservatively an increased level of 70 metres, the coast of southern England would have been dramatically different. East Anglia would have been mostly under water, most of Somerset submerged with Glastonbury Tor, Brent Knoll and Burrow Mump among the few outcrops, and the upper Severn valley an extremely broad waterway as the invading sea swept inland, making Worcestershire's Bredon Hill an island.

'Should we be surprised then that the early British established all their settlements, barrows and stones on the highest ground available?' asks Brooks. 'Is not a logical consequence that the hotbed of antiquity is to be found in Wiltshire which, surprisingly, is the English county with the highest average contour, having large high plateaux but few deep valleys? The lower marshy slopes would be an attractive habitat for sizeable reptiles and early civilised man would have had to share this hostile environment with marauding beasts and fearsome birds of prey. Could not his ditched and banked settlements have been defence against such wildlife rather than against the human neighbour who was equally constructive and bent upon a better life, just as we are today?'

Rather than elaborate tombs, chambered barrows could have had a more positive purpose as communal shelters for travellers. Standing stones, stone circles and smaller mounded tumuli were usually in isolated but prominent positions on the skyline and were easily spotted as sign-posts at the crossings of the ways.

Brooks's work, which so strongly emphasises the significance of Silbury Hill, complements that of Michael Dames, born 1939, a geogra-pher and archaeologist who, in his 1976 book 'The Silbury Treasure', was the first in modern times to identify the West Country landmark with the Great Goddess, as he calls her, or the Universal Mother, the female divi-nity worshipped in neolithic society.

Dames, shows that Silbury Hill, together with the carefully shaped quarry that surrounds it, is a massive landscape sculpture of the goddess, the hill itself representing the womb. In common with depictions of the Great Goddess in ancient art worldwide – in figurines and paintings on pottery – the figure is in the squatting position, as if ready to give birth. Belief in a squatting goddess, giving birth to the harvest in

August, continued in Britain long after the neolithic period ended at about 2000BC. The birth, according to Dames, was symbolised by the reflection of the full moon at a certain point in the moat on Lammas Eve (August 7). Dames also thus repudiates the conventional idea of Silbury Hill being a bronze age barrow, or burial mound, and laments vain efforts in the past to tunnel into the hill in search of treasure or ancient artefacts.

'The religion of the Great Goddess, celebrated at the Neolithic monuments in Avebury parish, including Silbury, was concerned with the three great realities of birth, marriage and death as they affected human, animal, vegetable and mineral events,' says Dames. 'It also sought to bring all together, within a harmonious universe, itself seen in human female form.'

It is not surprising that Silbury Hill, as a representation of the Great Goddess, should also be chosen as the hub of a far-reaching network of communication laid out by the neolithic geomancers with its inbuilt protective and 'homing' characteristics.

The purpose of geomancy in whatever guise was always related to the question of attaining or restoring balance in the environment by varying human pursuits so that they were in tune with the natural order and rhythm of nature rather than antagonistic to it, and that an advantageous poise was achieved between opposite forces to as great an extent as possible. It was founded on an intuitive, holistic world-view which accepted that all deeds and lifestyles were connected by a metaphysical pandect of correspondences, that any move which was made could have a noticeable impact on everything else.

It may be that this idea is the basis for the old belief in sympathetic magic, Jung's principle of synchronicity, and even today's ecological and New Age movements.

Most famous of the old Indian earthworks of North America, those sculpted into the shapes of enormous birds, men, and real or imaginary animals, is that of the serpent mound in Adams County, Ohio. The serpent is swallowing an egg, its tail ends in a perfect spiral, and its body has seven undulations, bringing together the traditional symbols of the earth spirit and of the ancient wisdom, and perhaps also relating to an astronomical event such as an eclipse.

The Mayans and the Aztecs were others who equated the earth spirit with a serpent-like creature (in fact, a kind of alligator) on whose back the world rested and, moreover, the snake or serpent god was nowhere more prevalent than in the early Central American civilisations in whose cultures the symbol was ubiquitously portrayed alongside the spiral

An impression of Silbury Hill, Wiltshire, showing the septenary spiral path to the summit believed to have been integral to the original construction of about 2500BC. Was it also the centre of an elaborate, spirally-designed navigational and settlement system?

from which it was derived. We can also see the serpent in the landscape at Avebury, in the form of the two megalithic avenues, Beckhampton and West Kennet, which stretch either side of the stone circle.

In ancient China, the natural energies proffered by the earth spirit were activated by the art of *feng-shui*, meaning literally 'wind and water', which was itself a form of geomancy, an attempt to balance the forces of yin and yang in the landscape, and to choose the most propitious places for the location of sacred buildings. Connected with this, and corresponding to the British leys, was the idea of *lung-mei*, or dragon paths (for the dragon or serpent symbolised the earth energies in the East too) along which the vital currents flowed, and the Chinese believed *lung-mei* covered the whole of the earth.

It could be that the dragon/serpent was also symbolic of movements in the Earth's crust, including earthquakes and volcanic eruptions, and that earth magic was an attempt to understand or placate these tectonic forces.

In 1977, the Dragon Project (named after the Chinese symbol for the earth force, or *ch'i*) was to bring together scientists, dowsers and various technical experts to assess energy effects, in the main, at one specimen megalithic site, the Rollright Stones in Oxfordshire.

The work of the project has shown that the energies previously only intuitively traced, by people whose sensibilities allowed them to 'feel out' the landscape in a rather mystical manner, can be registered as high frequency vibrations on electronic equipment, and that they seem to be able to cause surprisingly high readings on Geiger counters. One of the founders of the Dragon Project, Don Robins, an inorganic chemist and a researcher in archaeology, after five years of effort, concluded that 'stone circles do indeed emit anomalously high and anomalously low levels of several forms of radiation. Whatever they are, whatever purpose they serve, stone circles are not just points on a landscape' ('New Scientist', October, 1982).

Moreover, a survey reported later ('New Scientist', January, 1983) by retired BBC engineer Charles Brooker, revealed that as well as con-verging leys proper at the Rollright Stones, the magnetic pattern inside the stone circle formed a seven-ring spiral, broadening as it moved outward until it left the circle by the eastern gate. He also found a spiral of relative magnetic intensity – two stones on the west of the circle were pulsing magnetically, in cycles varying from 40–60 seconds.

While considering the possibility of such magnetic patterns, which perhaps helped to determine the layout of stone circles, there is evidence that the bluestones of Stonehenge, after they had been removed about

2000BC and later returned to be re-erected, were probably originally intended to form a spiral outside the Sarsen monument. Instead, the bluestones were finally erected as an inner circle and 'horseshoe' inside the Sarsen circle.

In 1983, the Dragon Project joined with the Association for the Scientific Survey of Anomalous Phenomena to launch the Gaia Programme, under which radiation was monitored at and near 30 sites and control locations. A much greater variation of readings at stone circles was found compared to the control locations, but long-term continuous monitoring was needed to discover any particular patterns or cycles in these variations. In 1987, the Dragon Project Trust was established to carry on the work and to study effects on consciousness at sites where actual geophysical anomalies had been pinpointed.

PATHS OF THE SERPENT

Peoples of the past recognised the way currents of energy seemed to snake and coil through the earth (and through the air too), leading to the use of the serpent and the winged dragon to symbolise them, bringing abundance to the places in the landscape that they touched, and being conspicuous by their absence in the places which they failed to nurture.

It is my conviction that the use of this symbolism derived from the collective unconscious which also identified the life-giving earth with the cosmic spiral of creation from which our planet was born billions of years ago.

The special properties of quartz have been suggested as a possible source of earth energy. Quartz is a naturally occurring silica and, found in pale-coloured veins in some rocks such as granite, it is one of the most widespread of minerals. In one form or another, it appears to be found in all standing stones, some of which actually have lumps of milky quartz sticking out from their surfaces.

In its smallest component it consists of three molecules of silicon dioxide arranged in a spiral or helicoid shape which can be right- or left-handed. Crystals of quartz display a lattice with a helical structure made up of silicon atoms linked with twice as many oxygen atoms – the lattice of a crystal having a strong influence on the larger forms in which a substance usually occurs. The diamond, a form of crystalline carbon, with its underlying cubical lattice, is a good example.

Some acids and salts, when seen in a ray of polarised light, exhibit spirals which turn either to the right or the left; and when two sections of quartz, one from a right-handed and the other from a left-handed crystal, both cut transversely to the vertical axis and placed one over the other, and similarly viewed, the phenomenon known as 'Airy's spirals' appears. Cinnabar (mercuric sulphide), a reddish ore which is the main source of mercury, is another example of a substance which has a crystal lattice with a helical structure. In this lattice, helical chains of alternating mercury and sulphur atoms similarly twist either to the right or the left. Cinnabar will rotate a plane of polarised light to a much greater extent than quartz.

Combining with various impurities, a whole series of quartzes are formed, including a wide variety of semi-precious crystals and stones such as chalcedony, amethyst, cairngorm, citrine, carnelian, onyx, agate, and flint, all of them silica derived. The magical use of such gems and crystals has been going on for thousands of years, and in this it seems more than coincidental that they should each be based on microscopic spiral forms.

In Taoism, cinnabar is probably the most potent symbolic natural substance of all, representing the cosmic energy of joined yin and yang, and related to immortality. The fortune teller's crystal ball, with which we are familiar today as a glass sphere, was in times past a globe polished from a large single crystal of quartz. Faience beads composed of a quartz core with a glass glaze, and which originated in the eastern Mediterranean almost 4,000 years ago, spread all over Europe, including Britain, and southern England in particular.

Crystals of quartz and white stones used to be placed in Irish graves; in Wales, offerings of white or quartz stones were made at holy wells; and both there and in Scotland charms of quartz and rock crystals were sought to give the water of healing wells a magical quality. The American indians and Australian aborigines held similar beliefs about the beneficence of quartz in the rituals of their medicine men.

Albertus Magnus, the 13th century Swabian alchemist, philosopher and magician, said that if quartz was placed in direct sunlight, and if cold, it would spurt fire. Here, possibly, is a more romantic origin for the term 'firestone', which is normally said to have gained its name, rather prosaically, through being used for lining hearths. Albertus was a keen observer of natural phenomena, and was captivated by the 'marvellous virtues' of stones and plants.

Most importantly, however, quartz is known for its piezo-electric properties. This means that crystals of clear quartz change their shape, expanding and contracting slightly, when subjected to an electric field, and when placed under pressure or tension, as they would be if charged while held inside stone, they exhibit electrical polarity and can emit negative and positive voltages on a surprising scale. These crystals are used in atomic clocks and for resonators and oscillators in radio and telecommunications.

Generally, the mineral has many applications nowadays, from cigarette lighters to wrist watches and computers, indeed, any electrical devices which need stable oscillators. A thin wafer properly cut from a crystal of quartz expands and contracts, or vibrates, when placed in a rapidly alternating electric field. It has a natural and constant frequency of vibration which on very thin plates may be many million times a second. When placed in an appropriate electrical circuit these quartz oscillator plates act as frequency controllers.

As silica, the basic compound on which all quartzes are based, is the most plentiful mineral in the earth's crust (silicon, after oxygen, is the most abundant element – although there is no adequate explanation as to why – and it crystallises in a diamond lattice) it comes as no surprise to find quartz common to standing stones. It is the odd mechano–electric properties of quartz that may explain the 'tingling' or 'charged' sensation which some people, especially dowsers, experience at standing stones, and the magnetic field effects which other investigators pick up in their vicinity.

The piezo-electric nature of quartz may allow another way of understanding the basis of the elusive natural energy apparently channelled along leys. Dowsing has shown that standing stones are positioned, in many instances, above underground water flows which could well be the origin of the vibrations which are found in them, and that some of the energies are linked to a lunar cycle indicating that gravitational effects can produce another regular change in the mechanical forces acting on certain stones. Different sizes and shapes of crystals in different stones might explain variations in energy levels.

It has been claimed that the amount of charge that can be produced in quartz is enough to affect the ionisation of the surrounding air so much that physiological changes can be caused in the bodies of living organisms nearby. It follows that quartz could have a potential in its vibrations, say Janet and Colin Bord, to restore a natural harmony to tissues and cells which are diseased, and that using pure well-water as a medium for conveying healing properties makes good sense – particularly, I would add, with that underlying spiral structure.

Quartz crystals can also be stimulated electronically to give off extremely high-frequency radio waves, called microwaves, which will pulse at regular intervals to produce a narrow beam. This is known as a maser beam – 'microwave amplification by stimulated emission of radiation'. The visible-light equivalent, working at a still-higher frequency, is, of course, the laser.

Herbert Weaver tells how, using Lawrence Veale's 'Revealer', a special kind of divining rod, he (Weaver) identified ray-paths of particle streams which linked an individual organism uniquely to dispersed portions over great distances, apparently by ionospheric reflection, as with radio signals. In his book, 'Divining the Primary Sense', Weaver records how Veale identified what he called 'paramagnetic suppressors' which control a chemical interchange between resonantly linked substances, and which can be arranged so as to either suppress or enhance radiations by using specifically geometered patterns of homogenous substances. This chemical interchange, Veale labelled 'homing conductance', because it homed in on the source of the radiation and conducted efficiently when at resonance.

Weaver, whose own theory (a development from dowsing) was that people, animals, plants and objects emit radiations that prehistoric and primitive man was able to sense directly, believed that rays linking deposits of identical inorganic chemical composition might be used over limited distances. One can easily see how his discovery can be applied to a kind of 'communication' between pieces of quartz, and especially those in standing stones aligned across the countryside and caused to vibrate either by underground streams or lunar cycles, or both, allowing us to see them perhaps as forms of megalithic masers.

'Revealer experiments show that chemicals, when oscillated by cosmic radiation, are linked in resonant interchange with their exactly co-oscillating chemical counterparts over considerable distances on the earth's surface,' said Weaver.

Wilhelm Reich (1897–1957) posited an 'orgone energy' which, as a fundamental sub-atomic force could be amplified into surging spiral patterns, and has been equated with earth energy. A pioneering psychiatrist, psychoanalyst and scientist, Reich's story is extraordinary. Born in Galicia, in the easternmost part of the Austro–Hungarian Empire, now Ukraine, he became a member of the Vienna Psychoanalytic Association in 1920, while at medical school. His recognition of the importance of sexuality had attracted him to the work of Freud, and Reich soon became one of the most active younger members of Freud's inner circle, and came to be looked on as one of Freud's most promising students.

In the 1930s, Reich claimed to have discovered a biological energy in all living matter which he labelled 'orgone', and for the next two decades he devoted his life to the investigation of its laws and properties. Moving to America in 1939, he bought an old farm a few miles from his cabin in

Maine in 1942, naming it Orgonon, and seeing it as a permanent home for his work. However, in 1954, the Food and Drug Administration filed an injunction against Reich in the Federal Court, stating that orgone energy did not exist, and asking the court to ban shipment of equipment and Reich's published literature. While Reich was away, and without his knowledge, one of his students, Dr. Michael Silvert, moved equipment and books from Maine to New York City, in direct violation of the injunction.

As a result, the FDA charged Reich and Silvert with criminal contempt of court. Following a jury trial, both men were found guilty in 1956. Reich was sentenced to two years in a federal prison, and Silvert was sentenced to a year and a day. The Wilhelm Reich Foundation, which was founded in Maine in 1949 by students and friends to preserve Reich's archives and to secure the future of his work, was fined $10,000.

Although Reich appealed against his sentence, the government destroyed his orgone accumulators and literature. In 1957, two weeks before his 60th birthday, Reich was temporarily held at the Danbury Federal Penitentiary in Connecticut, and then taken to the Federal Penitentiary at Lewisburg, Pennsylvania, where he died of heart failure.

> 'There is no need to go to the ends of the earth for interesting quests and excitement. It is here, anywhere in prosaic old England, at one's back door.'
>
> T C Lethbridge, *Gogmagog: The Buried Gods* (1956)

Another landscape phenomenon involving strange energy sources, which might well have intrigued Veale, Weaver and Reich, is that of the increasingly sophisticated and geometrically complex 'crop circles', or better, in many cases, crop spirals. Many thousands of these peculiar formations have been reported over the last 25 years, appearing not only in crops, but also in tree-tops, sand and ice, around the world, and giving rise to one of the most baffling phenomena of modern times.

One astonishing spiral pattern which appeared close to Stonehenge in July 1996 was made up of 151 separate circles of varying sizes, and, according to some, created itself within 15 minutes in broad daylight. Visitors to the spiral suddenly suffered headaches or found their cameras wouldn't work. Another pattern near Pewsey in Wiltshire in July 2002 was unmistakeably in the shape of an equiangular spiral 180ft across. Other crop spiral patterns have resembled the flow of stellar

The crop spiral which appeared near Stonehenge in July, 1996, made up of 151 separate circles.

material in spiral galaxies and the spirals carved at ancient chamber tombs and other megalithic sites.

It seems more than coincidence that a hallmark of the formations is that they so often appear near sites which ancient peoples regarded as sacred and where they founded their temples, stone circles, henges and so on, all with their connections to the spiral pattern. Indeed, Wiltshire, with its many ancient monuments, seems to be the crop circle capital of England, and the Wiltshire Crop Circle Study Group named their monthly newsletter 'The Spiral' after an enormous crop spiral which appeared at Beckhampton, near Avebury, in 1995 just as the group was being set up.

It is not known how many of these patterns are actual anomalies and how many are man-made, although any man-made ones would still be of significance, of course, because of the archetypal drive behind the desire to create them. Nevertheless, the increasing complexity of the designs seems to belie any notion of human artists or hoaxers. Scientific research has been minimal but it has been theorised that a new or as yet unclassified energy source, perhaps at the microwave level, could be creating some of the formations.

Biophysical and geological studies in the USA have discovered that soil at crop circle sites is heated to terrific temperatures of 500–1,500 degrees Celsius, with its molecular structure rearranged, and yet vegetation is not so much as singed. Plants taken from sites have also displayed curious changes involving the creation of tiny holes in the fibrous protuberances, or nodes, along the stem. It has been speculated that rapid heating causes moisture in the stems to turn to steam, suddenly blowing holes in the stems. This effect is seen only in the areas of vegetation which are flattened to create the pattern. Plant stems are gently bent horizontally, without any damage being caused in or around the patterned area, and the vegetation grows back normally afterwards.

Crop circles and spirals – and spirals could be the important clue here, bearing in mind the material presented in this book – may thus be intended to *communicate* something to us, perhaps by way of an expansion of our consciousness. There are various theories (beyond the scope of this book) as to what the message of the crop spirals might be, but who or what is behind the formations remains a mystery for the moment.

If one believes that the common uniting element of all creation is consciousness, that even the elementary particles contain units of it, then the spiral form promises a realisation of huge reservoirs of latent creative consciousness available to us.

THE DRAGON ISLE

'Glimpses of fair forgotten things
Beyond the gates of birth,
Half-caught from far off ancient springs
In heaven, and half of earth . . .'

Alfred Noyes (1880–1959), in *On the Downs*, from
The Enchanted Island

Lying off the south coast of England, the Isle of Wight is a place of many ancient secrets and is noted for its unique geology. There, a swathe of 'firestone', or upper greensand – such sandstones being composed chiefly of nodules of chalcedony and small quartz crystals – sweeps through the landscape in a shape resembling that of a formative spiral galaxy, hinting at the powerful natural energies of the island doubtless acknowledged by the adepts of old.

Indeed, I see the island as a prime exemplar of how the spiral curve in nature can manifest itself in the landscape in quite a dramatic manner and impinge itself on, or connect itself with, the environmental and cultural fabric of human communities. I call it the 'dragon isle' in reference to the Chinese concept of *lung-mei*, the 'dragon veins' which channel earth energies, and, of course, the dragon/serpent relationship to the spiral in antiquity, and we shall see how the dragon is a most appropriate symbol for this part of the world.

Spanning the island like the path of a spark or charge between the two terminals of an electrical generator, the band of firestone was noted by the 19th century Bonchurch poet Edmund Peel as appearing in the terrain like 'bars of sunshine across a dungeon shade'.

Incredibly, the very geological convulsion which formed the piece of land which became the island, with its own distinctive shape and geography, seems to have been determined by the forces of cosmic patterning. Since the 19th century, the island has been of special interest to conventional geologists, and no district of England of similar size has been held to be more interesting, from the grand variety of rock formations, the surprising merit of the geological exposures, and the abundance of fossils.

Here, the strata of southern England, although situated a little more than two miles from the mainland, have been raised up almost vertically through an angle of 90 degrees to appear side by side, just as if they had been prised into position by a lever of gargantuan size – this perhaps

94

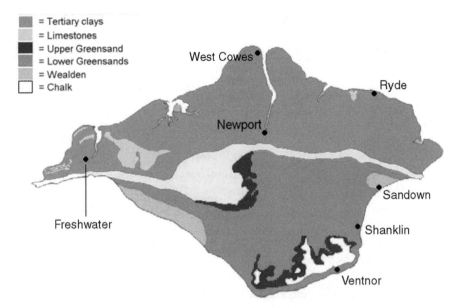

Geological map of the Isle of Wight showing the flattened 'S' pattern of the upper greensand, or 'firestone' stratum.

being part of the origin of the well-known Roman name for the island, Vectis, meaning 'lever', as in the act of lifting, suggesting land which has been raised above the sea. Fossils of fish, crocodiles, elephants and dinosaurs have been found, even of petrified trees, and at the western end of the island, at Alum Bay, the strata spill into view in an uncanny landscape of sands and clays arraying themselves in more than two dozen colours. The Solent, which separates the island from the mainland, was formed only about 8,000 years ago.

Remarkably, the ridge of firestone, which in folklore is known as the 'dragon's food', runs through the downs between the Nodes in the west of the island and Nodes Point in the east, these places positioned symmetrically like contact points. Nodes, the definition of which is also the meeting place of lines, roads or parts, from the Latin *nodus*, meaning a knot, may also act as valves controlling an energy flow, and this could be of particular importance when considering the nature of the firestone stratum.

Actually, 'node' or 'nodes' is a fairly common placename on the island, where it is used to describe a tumulus or burial mound, or a prominent sighting knoll from which one can get the 'lie of the land'. Near Godshill, for example, there is a Noddy Hill, and at Tennyson Down there is a Nodewell. The names may also have derived through the

Old English *hnod*, meaning a knoll or hill, or from the Old Norse *nod*, which means a lump.

Bronze Age burial mounds lie in profusion on and around the downs, which were once traversed by a prehistoric highway winding from Brading to Freshwater Bay. More than 240 mounds have been identified, almost all of them on the chalk down. Some have been ploughed under and others are covered with trees. One barrow on Gallibury Down was excavated in 1979–80, and material from graves and pits under it was radio-carbon dated to between 1600–1400BC.

As part of the uptilted strata, the firestone coils in a serpentine loop across the island, not only reminiscent of the shape of nascent spiral galaxies, and sculpting from the terrain the semblance of a huge yin-yang symbol, but also mirroring the apparent retrograde motion of the Moon as it crosses the ecliptic (the Sun's apparent orbit). Once again, we are reminded of the Hermetic axiom: as above, so below.

In astronomy, the nodes are the points where the apparent path of the Moon crosses the ecliptic, but because of the way the Moon moves about the Earth its apparent path through the ecliptic is a flattened S-shape which ancient astrologers and geomancers likened to that of a dragon. The north node of the Moon was called Caput Draconis, the dragon's head, and the south node, Cauda Draconis, the dragon's tail, and the two points were among the 16 traditional figures of geomancy. The former was also related to the constellation of Draco, the dragon.

Cauda Draconis has as its divinatory meanings the lower kingdom or outer threshold, and represents the harbinger of disaster; Caput Draconis refers to the entrance or upper kingdom. Appearing at either end of the firestone heights, these points symbolise the descending and ascending spiral movements, respectively, of spirit to matter and of matter to spirit.

Imagine, therefore, the latent or potential energy in this swathe of firestone and quartz. The stratum, bordered on one side by Gault clays and on the other by middle and lower chalk formations which also follow the serpentine shape, runs from Culver Cliff, the 'head of the dragon', west through Brading (where the 12th century parish church stands on a rock of white sandstone) and Arreton Down. Here, according to an island legend, Stonehenge once stood and acted as a Druid temple.

The band sweeps across St George's Down, below which stands St George's Church, Arreton, inside which is to be found a dragon's head of carved stone, a totem linked locally with the legend of St George and the Dragon, and originally built into the north wall of the church together with a statue of the saint.

At a point close to Carisbrooke Castle, the stratum swings back to the south-east to Gatcombe, and then curves back to the west through Chillerton, where there is an Iron Age camp said to have been the island's tribal centre, to Shorwell, Brook Down, and on towards the Needles which, with the striking appearance of giant vertebrae jutting out of the sea, are strong contenders for the 'tail of the dragon', if only in metaphor.

The emblem of Freshwater parish, adjacent to the Needles, portrays a winged dragon riding on water. It is identical to a seal presented to the village by one of its illustrious residents, the great English visionary Alfred Lord Tennyson. It is not clear why Tennyson favoured this design, but one could put it down to poetic intuition.

On the downs a few miles from Freshwater stands the 15ft Longstone, or the Mottistone as it has also been called, giving its name to the village below. It is the oldest man-made structure on the island and, as 'the stone of Meeting rear'd by pagan hands', it pre-dates the Pyramids. A pure spring, the Buttlehole, once rose nearby.

The Longstone is one of only three surviving field monuments of the neolithic period on the island, the others being a long barrow on Afton Down and a 'mortuary enclosure' on Tennyson Down. At the foot of the Longstone, a 9ft stone lies fallen, this having been moved from a location a short distance away, facing the sunrise at summer solstice, in the 19th century by a landowner who wanted to see what was underneath, but found nothing. A small archaeological excavation at the Longstone in 1956 did not locate any burials.

Just to the west of the Longstone, on the scarp slope of the downs, and positioned along the edge of the firestone ridge, is a 70ft submegalithic long barrow lying ESE–WSW, suggesting an orientation to sunrise at the summer solstice, an alignment used in the construction of temples and monuments throughout the ancient world, including Stonehenge, the main axis of which points to this annual event when crowds still gather to see the sun come up over the Heel Stone. It is thought that the Longstone and the fallen stone once formed the portal to the adjacent long barrow. Nearby, to the south-east, there is another Iron Age hillfort, and the biggest round barrow on the island, the Black Barrow, is about a kilometre due east.

As implied by the name Mottistone, which means 'speaker's stone' in Old English, the Longstone has been thought of as a meeting place of the Celts, who believed in an endless cycle of birth, death and rebirth, and of their elite class, the Druids. Legend has it that it was here that the Druids sacrificed white bulls to the Sun – Osiris, the Egyptian god which inspired Druidism, was referred to as a bull. The bull was not only the symbolic animal of Druidism but also of Mithraism which involved ceremonies in which initiates subjected themselves, as in Druidism, to a symbolic death and were then reborn, calling to mind once again spirality as the symbol of regeneration.

In St Olave's Church at Gatcombe there is a lifesize effigy of a knight carved from the trunk of an oak (the Druids' sacred tree), reputed to be a memorial to Sir Ralph de Gorges, a Crusader who, in the 13th century, acquired an estate at Knighton, below the rim of the downs, and near an important Iron Age site not far from Alverstone. By marriage, Sir Ralph also came into large estates in Dorset and Somerset.

He was Sheriff of Devon and later governor of Sherborne, 'a military man and engaged in all the wars of those times', and he accompanied Prince Edward to the Holy Land. Ralph fought at the siege of Caerlaverock Castle, near Dumfries in 1300, when Edward, now king, was on one of his expeditions to conquer and subdue the Scottish nation. We are told that, in the fighting, Sir Ralph fell 'more than once to the ground from stones and the crowd, for he was of so haughty a spirit that he would not deign to retire'.

Sir Ralph was the son of Ivo de Gorges, believed to have been sixth in descent from the Norman Ralph or Ranulph de Gorges who came to England with William the Conqueror. He had a deer park at Litton in Dorset, a castle at Powerstock and a manor at Shipton Gorge which still bears his name.

It is significant that his Isle of Wight estate at Knighton straddles the firestone stratum for Sir Ralph had for his coat of arms the heraldic device 'gurges', from the Latin for whirlpool, traditionally an azure spiral on silver, while Sir Ralph's spiral emblem was azure on gold. It is thought the family may have derived their name from a hamlet in Lower Normandy and, according to John Hutchins, for a time the Rector of Swyre, in his 'History of Dorset', the family took the mystical 'gurges' for their arms in allusion to that placename.

However, later Mascally or lozengy and azure was used, the latter said to have been that of the Morvilles with whom the Gorges had united in marriage. Yet certain of Sir Ralph's descendants still incorporated 'gurges' in their arms. In the coats of arms of the Morvilles and the Gorges, in Mascally or lozengy and in 'gurges', the diamond and spiral patterns are linked.

The 'gurges' device links de Gorges to the esoteric practices of the Knights Templar who were founded as a crusading order at the beginning of the 12th century and drew their inspiration from mystical

'Gurges', from the Latin for whirlpool, the heraldic device of the de Gorges family.

Judaism and Islam which they had encountered in the Holy Land, as well as the Cathars, an heretical Christian sect whose creed broadly conformed to ancient Gnostic and Mithraic doctrines concerning the indeterminate struggle between light and darkness.

By the beginning of the 14th century, both the Templars and the Cathars had been liquidated by the Catholic Church as 'Satanic' men. For the Templars, however, the spiral may certainly have been the guardian symbol of a spiritual journey, similar to that already described in relation to the maze, but perhaps also borrowed from the Great Seal of Solomon.

The Templars, who vowed to devote themselves to the protection of Christian shrines and routes of pilgrimage, were formed under the original name of the Poor Knights of Christ and the Temple of Solomon, but they gained their more familiar name, according to some, through being quartered in buildings next to the site of the Temple in Jerusalem. More likely, perhaps, the name relates to their aim, as builders as well as soldiers, of rebuilding the Temple of Solomon for, as Eliphas Levi pointed out, the Temple had actually ceased to exist before the knights came on the scene.

The Templars came to rule large estates and collect tribute all over western Europe, including Britain. In Chartres Cathedral, where there is a medieval ritual maze drawn on the flagstones inside, the stained glass window of St Denis depicts a Templar praying before a spiral motif. In 'Parzival', the German quest epic of 1210, by Wolfram von Eschenbach, a mystical knighthood called Templars are named as the keepers of the Holy Grail, long said to be the sacred vessel of the Last Supper, or the container(s) of Christ's blood and sweat following the crucifixion. While this poem is only indirect evidence of the Templars' connection with the Grail, it is interesting to note that in this text the knights regard the Grail as a restorer of youth and the secret of the Phoenix' rebirth.

Joseph of Arimathea, the uncle of Jesus, was said to have taken the Grail to Glastonbury where terraces around the Tor may be the remains of a three-dimensional maze, providing a further possible explanation for the de Gorges crest which, in turn, points to the possible guardianship of the Grail by the Templars. The Apprentice Pillar in the Rosslyn Chapel – the 'Second Temple of Solomon' – near Edinburgh, the building of which has been linked with the Knights Templar, is decorated with spirals of leaves and other carvings, identifying it as a representation of the Tree of Life, a synonym for Christ in Christian iconography, and the pillar also has eight coiled serpents around its base.

Sir Ralph was not the Isle of Wight's only link with the Templars. At Brook, in the West Wight, there was a family called Maskerel who, in the 12th century, were benefactors of the Templars and of Quarr Abbey. After the Templars were extinguished, the family's property passed to the Knights Hospitallers who kept the lands until after the monasteries were suppressed by Henry VIII. The de Gorges family evidently died out in England in the 17th century, leaving only one branch extant in Ireland in the 19th century, but their Isle of Wight estate continues to be known as Knighton Gorges to this day.

Just outside the door of All Saints' Church at Godshill stands an 18th century gravestone decorated with a double spiral pattern, there as if to acknowledge Godshill's connections with the dragon force embracing the island. Inside the church, there is a portrait and a statuette of St George and the Dragon, a traditional rood beam with the foot of the cross crushing a rather ferocious wyvern – a winged dragon with a barbed tail – and a stained glass window depicting St Michael. There is even a wyvern weathervane on the church tower.

The wyvern links the church to the Worsley family who, early in the 16th century, acquired the Appuldurcombe estate, about a mile and a half south of Godshill, and took the winged dragon (standing for strength and power) for their crest. The church has several monuments to the family, and their wyvern is also found depicted on a number of buildings in the locality, including the Fremantle Gate, an Ionic triumphal archway which stands at the end of an old carriage track from Godshill to the edge of the former Appuldurcombe lands.

Appuldurcombe House, the building of which was begun by Sir Robert Worsley in the first decade of the 18th century and completed by his grandson Richard in the seventh, had 365 windows, 53 rooms and seven staircases. Above the east-facing main entrance was a circular 'bull's-eye' window through which the rays of the morning sun, as it rose over St Martin's Down opposite the house, illuminated the Great Hall within.

According to legend, Christian missionaries began to build a church on flat ground about a mile from the present village of Godshill. On three successive occasions, and in the manner of similar legends concerning the siting of a number of British churches, the stones were removed mysteriously at night to the site of the present church, atop a steep-sided hill where once had stood a pagan shrine. This may well be a folk memory of how the proper geomantic location of the church was achieved.

When the church was finished, so the story goes, 'great rejoicings and sounds of mirth' were heard, commonly attributed to the 'little people' celebrating the occasion. Another local folktale describes the knoll on which the church stands as the 'iron hill', the interior of which was inhabited by elves who mined iron ore. The hill is actually composed of 'ironsand', or ferruginous sands, which also underlie the whole of the countryside around Godshill.

The story of the elves is of a kind associated with many mystical sites and 'fairy hills' in Britain and Ireland, and confirms that long ago people were extremely respectful of the church hill at Godshill and revered it as a place of spirits. It is said, rather charmingly, that male gnomes wore pointed hoods symbolising 'above', while female gnomes wore hoods in a spiral shape symbolising 'within'.

The present All Saints' Church is the fourth on the site, being rebuilt from one of similar design, and preceded by Norman and Saxon buildings of which there is scant trace today. It is evident that there has been a church on the hill for more than 900 years. The old English 'godeshyll' may simply have meant 'holy hill', or denoted a pagan cult centre for the worship of a number of gods.

As Albin's 'History of the Isle of Wight' (1796) says, it is probable that 'on some account or other the hill was honoured by its present appellation anterior to the building of the church. This conjecture is strengthened by a superstitious tradition of great antiquity'.

It is entirely conceivable that, as at Glastonbury Tor, the church hill at Godshill was recognised as a point where earth energies were concentrated, and that a three-dimensional maze was laid out around the hill, following the classical labyrinth model, and turning it into a 'spiral castle', as Taliesin would have described such a centre of ancient mystery. It comes as no surprise, then, to find that the hill is a nodal point in the local ley system, with leys radiating from here to sites of antiquity in all parts of the island. Such points are special, and promise a kind of link between two worlds, where prayers can be heard and given response.

After all, rituals integrating man with the natural world, relating macrocosm to microcosm, were extremely common on the Isle of Wight until quite recent times. These were the gyratory dances connected with geomantically positioned maypoles which symbolised the annual spinning of the heavens about the earth. Maypoles were formerly set up on all village greens on the island, and islanders excelled in maypole dances for hundreds of years. The patterns traced on the ground by the dancers, as they gradually approached the centre-pole with the ribbons intertwining, are duplicated in the convolutions of the labyrinths, the paths of which lead from the outer to the inner worlds.

It may also be significant that the tower of All Saints' Church, a landmark for miles around, is one of the towers most frequently struck by lightning in the country. It is known to have been struck severely three times, in 1778, 1897 and 1904. J G Frazer, in 'The Golden Bough', pointed out that the places where lightning struck, certainly in Europe, were considered sacred, the lightning giving them a 'nimbus of glory'.

Church towers or standing stones could actually be made to glow in the charge surrounding them, gathered during a thunderstorm from streams in the ground beneath. They could act as veritable lightning conductors, allowing conduction from both sky to land, and land to sky, carrying a lightning strike to earth, or counteracting a charge in a thundercloud.

Dowsers have found that in open countryside lightning often strikes on the junction of water lines, whether underground streams or simply water-carrying fissures. This is because a bolt of lightning is a huge electrical charge attempting to find the quickest way of discharging itself, and this means locating the speediest route of greatest conductivity in its immediate area.

Would it not be reasonable to assume that the All Saints' hill, veined with subterranean water, was also often struck by lightning in the times before the first church was built there, the 'fireflash' providing the people of those days with added evidence of the sacred nature of the site and of its qualities as a connecting point between Earth and Heaven?

Guy Underwood suggested that the orientation of Christian churches, and not merely prehistoric sites, was determined by telluric currents, and he found that a strong spring was often located directly under a tower. This could also help to explain the number of lightning strikes at Godshill.

A picture of the Isle of Wight as a huge earth 'oscillator', powered by the lunar and solar cycles, channelling earth energies, and offering sanctuary and magical powers, is suggested by the firestone 'spark gap', and complemented by the lozenge, or conventional diamond, shape of the island, a mystical shape repeated in the stones of Avebury Circle and its adjacent Kennet Avenue in Wiltshire.

Millennia ago, the island must have had an even more noticeable diamond shape prior to the coastal erosion which has since taken place. Indeed, the island's shape most closely corresponds to two equilateral triangles joined together, the equilateral triangle being one of the most basic structural forms in nature, from crystals to honeycombs.

Herbert Weaver demonstrated that such a shape in nature, or applied by man, afforded wide protection against 'the dangers of the profane world and also shielded man against the unpredictable malice of a higher, capricious god who was responsible for nature's cataclysms'. Dylan Thomas, that 'Druid of the broken body', in a return to an emphasis on the physical substance of language, used the diamond shape as a womb/birth symbol in his visual poem 'Vision and Prayer'.

In the very structure of the Isle of Wight, then, where the dragon energies of eternal creation must still course through the landscape, the two great safeguarding symbols of antiquity, the spiral and the diamond, come together on an impressive scale,

'... you can spend days and days and days exploring the Isle of Wight, which, if you are really interested, begins magically enlarging itself for you.'

J B Priestley (1894–1984), *The Shell Guide to England*

5

The Spiraculate Universe

'And, burning ciphers on the round of space,
Heaven and hell mixed as they spun.'

Dylan Thomas (1914–53), *In the beginning*

The theory for the origin of the universe which has been given credence by the majority of scientists has been that of the Big Bang, or 'standard' or 'consensus' model, as it has often been termed, a cataclysm of unimaginable intensity which took place some 20 billion years ago and which, as the turbulent gas of sub-atomic particles which was given off cooled and eddied into galaxies of stars, eventually resulted in the formation of our own Sun, the Earth and the other planets. The theory states that at a time in the unimaginably distant past there was simply nothing, but a process known as vacuum fluctuation created what astrophysicists call a singularity, and from that singularity, about the size of a 10p coin, our universe was born.

The gas, by the nature of its turbulence in unrestricted space, acquired localised compressions and imbalances, and once the particles were compressed in this way, gravitational attraction between them was able to increase, and 'clumps' of immense size, with masses millions of times greater than that of the Sun, appeared.

The larger the clump, the greater the gravitational force pulling the particles ever closer together – too large, and the relentless gravitational whirlpool, collapsing continually inwards on itself, would create a black hole; but if smaller, centrifugal force would arrest the contraction and random motions within it would make it rotate, in the manner of an eddy, with an increasing speed that would cast material away from the direction of spin, forming spiral appendages. In the centre of the eddy, collapse would continue until the structure flattened into the disc of a spiral galaxy, like our own Milky Way.

It is extremely difficult to imagine the very earliest moments of the universe as it was exploding into existence. Physical laws as we understand them were not in existence due to the presence of fantastically large quantities of energy, in the form of photons. Some of the photons became quarks, and the quarks formed neutrons and protons. After a time, large numbers of hydrogen, helium and lithium nuclei were created. Theoretical assessments of the amounts and types of elements formed during the Big Bang have been made and they seem to agree with observed phenomena.

In 1965, astronomers found their first convincing evidence that the universe was expanding. Static picked up on a radio antenna turned out to be microwave radiation left over from the beginning of time, indeed, an echo of the Big Bang. This cosmic microwave background (CMB) provided a snapshot of what the universe was like only 300,000 years after the Big Bang and was mapped by a team at Berkeley in the early 1990s.

But when astronomers looked at it closely they encountered a problem. The radiation appeared in uniform manner from all directions, suggesting there was no discernable centre to the cosmos, which seemed to go against the idea that the universe expanded in proportion to time from a particular point of origin.

Scientists also realised that, as it appeared, the universe should have collapsed on itself soon after the Big Bang from the force of its own gravity. It is extremely difficult to explicate how, some time after the Big Bang, clumps of matter were condensed together, gravitationally pulled towards other clumps, and eventually formed galaxies, but most models agree that it occurred faster than it should have. A possible answer to the problem is that the size of the early universe greatly increased in a very short period of time, beginning as an incredibly hot and dense speck of matter and energy, and then exploding with particles flying outward faster than the current speed of light.

Didn't Albert Einstein (1879–1955) say that the speed of light could not be exceeded? Well, the new theory gets round that because Einstein's law restricted the speed of things travelling along the fabric of space–time, whereas the idea here is that the fabric itself, which is not subject to Einstein's rule, expanded faster than the speed of light.

The explanation is known as inflation theory and, although the theory is simple and elegant, it is as yet unverifiable, but its mathematics are sound and it has become widely accepted among astrophysicists because of its ability to explain some of the difficulties with the Big Bang scenario, and because it reconciles theory with observation. It explains not only what caused the universe to expand, but also the origin of virtually all the matter in the universe. The theory was published by MIT physics professor Alan Guth in 1981, and in 2002, he and fellow cosmologists Paul Steinhardt and Andrei Linde were awarded the Dirac Medal of the International Centre for Theoretical Physics for the development of the concept.

Guth says: 'The inflationary-universe theory is an add-on to the standard Big Bang theory, and basically what it adds on is a description of what drove the universe into expansion in the first place. In the classical version of the Big Bang theory, that expansion was part of the initial assumptions; there's no explanation for it whatsoever. The classical theory was never really a theory of a bang; it was a theory about the aftermath of a bang.'

A period of rapid, or exponential, transition of the universe is now thought to have happened 10–35 seconds after creation, filling the universe with a type of energy known as vacuum energy, the density of which caused gravitation effectively to become repulsive for 10–32 seconds. At this moment, the universe expanded at an amazing rate, increasing its size by about a factor of 1,050. When the phase finished, the universe settled down into the Big Bang development previously envisaged by scientists before the advent of inflation theory, the laws of physics took over, and the universe continued to grow at the speed of light.

The staggering implication of this is that the entire volume of the universe which we have been able to observe to date – which is about 18 billion light years into space – expanded from a volume only a few centimetres across when inflation got under way.

But most importantly for the study of spirals, inflation theory, as well as solving problems with the Big Bang, pays an extra dividend. Detailed computations have indicated that inflation is capable of producing small density fluctuations which, later in the evolution of the universe, can provide the means for matter to begin clumping together to form the spiral galaxies and other structures.

'. . . the stellar constellations themselves, and the almost mathematical symmetry of the spiral nebulae, are examples of forms and structures that recur time after time throughout the universe, as though there were identical moulds throughout space into which the matter of the universe had been poured'.

Professor Lloyd Motz,
The Universe: its Beginning and End, 1976

Cosmologists were initially puzzled by the mechanics which supported the majestic spiral arms attached to at least 80 per cent of galaxies, and about which invisible magnetic fields spiralled also. Spiral galaxies have markedly flattened distributions of matter characterised by a central plane where stars form in spiral patterns, evidence of enormous waves of alternating dense and rarefied gas which are in orbit about the centre. Gas that does not immediately contribute to the creation of star clusters drops to the galactic plane, accumulating a disc of material which is stockpiled for star formation later.

For billions of years in the past, and for billions more years in the future, spiral galaxies will continue to manufacture stars, each successive generation more endowed with heavy elements (those heavier than helium and which are essential for the formation of planets) than the one before. A theory of turbulence coupled with rotation has been put forward to explain the formation of our solar system from condensations and accretions of gas and dust, the planets being created by eddies of this material within one huge revolving gaseous cloud.

In the elliptical centre of a spiral galaxy are older, or first generation stars, while the stars of the disc and the spiral arms themselves are younger, later additions to the basic structure, and it could be that galaxies forming initially as ellipticals have the potential to grow into spirals of different shapes and sizes. According to the astrophysicists C C Lin and W W Roberts, of the University of California, the pattern into which a galaxy settles is sometimes similar to that of a turbulent flow: a flow of fluid dominated by large-scale motions but with smaller scales superposed within. NASA researchers Rubi Mehta and Dan McKernan took this cue ('New Scientist', February, 1984) to propose a close resemblance between spiral galaxies and real whirlpools, such as the flow of water down a plughole.

They did not believe this resemblance was coincidental; the origin of galaxies was often modelled in terms of fluid flow, they pointed out, continuing: 'The dark and narrow dust lanes which form the spiral pattern may be related to shock waves formed in the gaseous component of the galaxy, and the spiral pattern itself is believed to be a wave moving around the galaxy which triggers the formation of new stars where pressure is high.'

They said the driving force for this galactic whirlpool was gravity, which affected the gaseous fluid much more than the stars themselves. Using a wind tunnel and streams of air, they created spiral patterns, the flows of which showed detailed similarities to that of a galaxy. Although the forces in the wind tunnel experiment did not include gravity, the pair believed the image could provide insights into the way galaxies formed.

Stars such as the Sun have been produced by the collapse of gas clouds which have already been processed at least once through the explosions of earlier stars to produce heavy elements. First generation stars would have been without any planets because these heavy elements would not yet have been made by nuclear fusion in the stellar 'factories'. One explanation is that these clouds built up over hundreds of millions of years from thinner concentrations of material through repeated transit across the 'compression lanes' of gas and dust bordering the spiral arms.

A cloud of gas in orbit about the galactic centre would pass through these lanes until its density was great enough for collapse to continue under its own gravity, and for stars to be born. The action of these 'density waves' prevents the spiral arms from eventually folding up against the faster rotating inner parts of the galactic disc, as one would otherwise expect, and explains why the arms are so long-lived. The birth of new stars continually renews the spiral formation, delineating the denser sections of stellar material in the disc. Gravitational forces caused by the asymmetric distribution of matter in the galaxy perturbs the motion of stars and gas clouds and generates a spiral density wave.

Molecular astronomers have been able to identify many organic chemicals drifting about in the dust and gas of our galaxy's spiral arms. In the continuing process of the birth and death of stars, these ingredients, in addition to the hydrogen and other elements in these arms, are incorporated into the planets and stars of new solar systems. In just such a way, our solar system was formed, and the materials from which life could be created were similarly incorporated into the primordial Earth, and subsequently into all living creatures on it.

Our solar system came into being as a direct result of the spirality of our home galaxy, the Milky Way, and the arms of spiral galaxies are the birthplaces of stars whose attendant planets are capable of seeing the evolution of life. We are, therefore, the spiral's spawn, and the abundance of spiral galaxies signifies the promise of life elsewhere in the cosmos.

It has long been known that our own Milky Way galaxy is a spiral but, in August 2005, astronomers at the University of Wisconsin–Madison announced that there is something very special about it, bearing in mind the high proportion of spiral galaxies in the universe. According to an exhaustive survey of stars in the middle of the galaxy by astronomers and physicists including professors Edward Churchwell and Robert Benjamin, the Milky Way has a characteristic central bar feature about 27,000 light years long which marks it out from most

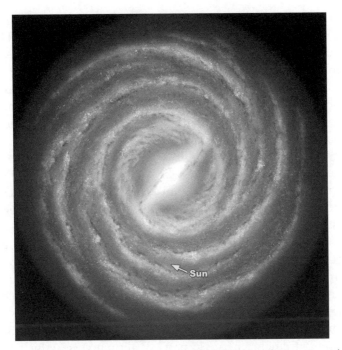

The new impression of our Milky Way galaxy, produced from a survey by scientists at the University of Wisconsin–Madison in 2005.

other spiral galaxies. The survey was carried out using NASA's orbiting infra-red Spitzer space telescope, and sampled light from about 30 million stars in the plane of the galaxy so as to build up a detailed picture of the inner regions of the Milky Way.

The possibility of a stellar bar at the centre has been considered before by astronomers, as bars are clearly evident in other galaxies, and there has been debate as to whether a central feature of our galaxy would be a bar structure or an ellipse, or both. Now, the Wisconsin study has given best estimates for the size and orientation of a bar which are much different from earlier suggestions. The bar appears to consist of relatively old and red stars, its length of 27,000 light years being 7,000 light years longer than previously thought. It also shows that the bar is oriented at about 45 degrees to a line joining the Sun and the galactic centre.

'All things come from the originative process of Nature and return to the originative process of Nature'.

Chuang Tzu, Taoist philosopher, 4th century BC

During the existence of the universe, matter may leak in and out through cosmic spiracles called black holes and white holes. The black hole extracts matter from the universe in a locally irresistible gravitational whirlpool in space–time. Meanwhile, the white hole pours matter back into the universe in a gushing cataract and, according to the astrophysicist John Gribbin who put forward this theory, can actually create the galactic spiral – 'a veritable melting pot for redistributing the elements' and bringing about the conditions under which life can begin.

Astronomers tend to see a black hole – where an old star collapses to such a state in which intense gravity stops anything, including light, from getting away into space – as a beginning rather than an ending. If matter can go spiralling into a black hole, perhaps it can emerge from a white hole, and maybe there are even tunnels through space and time which connect black and white holes, connecting either two points in hypothetical different universes, or two points in our own universe.

It is still not yet known whether these cosmic time-tunnels do actually exist, and if they do, how they could continue to remain open, and whether they could offer routes to other locations in space and time. Conjecture about the existence of white holes goes a long way to explain the extremely energetic parts of the universe which appear to be spraying out matter from tiny points, and speculation is certainly founded on proven scientific reasoning.

However, astronomers generally accept that most galaxies conceal a huge black hole at their centres, and that they have masses millions or even billions of times greater than that of our Sun. It is believed that a black hole of about three million solar masses lies at the heart of our Milky Way. The 'event horizon' of such a black hole – the point at which light can no longer escape from the black hole due to the tremendous gravitational forces, making it impossible for us to see into it – would be about eight million kilometres across, a great deal smaller than the distance between the Earth and the Sun. Therefore, we need have no concerns about being dragged down into our own local cosmic whirlpool any more than being sucked into a mythological maelstrom near the coast of Norway!

However, with billions of galaxies in the universe, each with hundreds of billions of stars, we have an enormous range of black holes available to investigate, and a number of space missions, which will involve the launching of orbiting satellites with special telescopes, are planned for this very purpose in coming years. For example, there is the proposed Supernova Acceleration Probe, a satellite which would use an extremely hi-tech camera to photograph the skies in the hope of locating supernovae – exploding stars. It would reap a rich harvest of information about galaxies as well and allow astrophysicists to work out the rate of the expansion of the universe over aeons.

Observation has revealed that the galaxies are flying apart as the universe continues to expand from the thrust of the initial explosion, the most optimistic, philosophically and symbolically satisfying implication of which is that at some time the momentum of the outflying galaxies – which were first noted by Edwin Hubble in the 1930s – must expend itself and that the galaxies will then start falling back to their point of origin, finally crushing together in a 'singularity', or Big Crunch – a geometrical point of no size yet of gigantic mass – to erupt through another 'big blowhole' and give rise to a new universe.

The idea is that this evolutionary cyclic process of expansion–contraction–explosion, or birth–death–rebirth, could go on forever, introducing an endless series of spiracular universes in an eternal breathing in and breathing out of space–time. From this theory comes the attractive conclusion that matter is not draining away into bottomless black holes but is constantly recycled, with a universe always rising Phoenix-like from its own ashes and promising a kind of eternal life.

Within each cosmic cadenza, then, lies the seed of a new universe. An agreement about affirmations of rebirth can be found in the most widely differing societies the world over, such affirmations surely counting among the primordial assertions of humankind. As Jung pointed out, the mere fact that there is a concept of rebirth at all means that a store of psychic experiences described by that term must actually exist. The spiral is its symbol.

A number of cosmologists, including Alexander Friedmann, Robert Dicke and George Gamow, have seriously considered the cyclic model. Indeed, another aspect of inflation theory, discussed above, is that it shows that the universe does not have to be unique; it predicts that myriad universes have been created and are being created all the time, and can therefore be used to support the idea of a cyclic universe. The idea of 'eternal inflation', which Guth accepts and on which Linde has done much work, permits the occurrence of many Big Bangs. Whether these would be alike, or whether the material in each of them would be subject to different laws, is not known.

Of course, the 'recycling' theory is not the only idea which scientists have put forward about what might be the fate of the universe in the far distant future: other theories see the universe expanding forever, although gradually slowing down, or its expansion simply coming to a halt at some stage. The three scenarios were, in fact, put forward by Friedmann as long

The M51 spiral galaxy.

ago as the 1920s. In the late 1990s, some cosmologists, who were studying the rate at which certain supernovae were moving away from us, came up with a fourth option, that the expansion of the universe was actually speeding up – evidence for the speed-up was that explosions of distant stars were fainter than had been expected.

The power behind this acceleration was called 'dark energy', the term 'dark' indicating that the nature of this energy was, and still is, unknown – and yet it accounts for an amazing 70 per cent of the total mass and energy in the universe. It is thought that the 'dark energy' might be a constant energy density which arises from the vacuum (Einstein's 'cosmological constant'), or a hypothetical field which varies in space and time and has been dubbed 'quintessence'. Indeed, only five per cent of the universe is composed of the 'ordinary' matter with which we are familiar here on our own planet.

As well as 'dark energy', most of the universe also comprises 'dark matter' which has been detected through observation of stars and galaxies which has shown that they are being pulled this way and that by the gravitational forces of other matter which is invisible to us, due to the fact that it does not emit light. This 'dark matter' could be made up of a new range of sub-atomic particles yet to be discovered and named by science because at present they cannot be found on Earth. There is five times more 'dark matter' in the universe than there is ordinary matter.

'The results of scientific research very often force a change in the philosophical view of problems which extend far beyond the restricted domain of science itself.'

Albert Einstein and Leopold Infeld,
Evolution of Physics, 1938

It is possible that our universe may have been created by a black hole in another universe. The idea is that such a singularity wrenches itself loose from its parent universe and inflates, turning into a universe of its own. In this way, our universe could be continually giving birth to infant universes.

Natural symmetry in the universe allowed the concept of the white hole to follow on that of the black, as the notion of anti-matter followed from the study of the sub-atomic composition of matter. Particle physics, as if opening a series of Chinese boxes, has gradually discovered that smaller and smaller particles go to make up matter, progressing from the atom to the nucleus to the proton to the quark, even to the graviton. Hundreds of elementary particles, and their corresponding anti-particles, have been identified and their origins traced back to the Big Bang in which they, and then the nuclei and atoms, necessary for the construction of matter, were generated.

These discoveries have enabled physicists not only to understand much of the sub-atomic phenomena themselves but allowed them to use the properties of the sub-atomic particles to explain many larger-scale phenomena which previously were inexplicable, such as the origin of the Sun's energy and the chemical properties of the elements in the universe.

These elements, which today number 115, are represented in the Periodic Table which the Russian chemist Dmitry Mendeleyev (1834–1907) put together in 1869 from the 63 elements then known to exist. He arranged the elements in rows and columns, which enabled the discovery of missing elements to be forecast, but he thought the table could be best represented by a cylindrical helix, although that would have required a three-dimensional figure. Significantly, chemists before and after Mendeleyev proposed a spiral arrangement of the table to obtain the benefits of a helix in two dimensions and better show the relationships between the elements. In 1960, the table was indeed redrawn convincingly as a spiral by the German organic chemist Otto Theodor

Benfey in a radical departure from the conventional diagram. In 2005, a British scientist, Philip Stewart, an ecologist at the University of Oxford, took the spiral Periodic Table a stage further by radiating the elements from a central point against the background of a spiral galaxy. In Stewart's 'Chemical Galaxy', the elements spiral outward in a continuous progression, from the lowest to the highest atomic number, improving the table's 'flow', spokes of the spiral corresponding to the columns in the old table. This new vision of the Periodic Table gives expression to the astronomical dimension of chemistry and, said Stewart, was also designed to 'evoke wonder at the order underlying the universe'.

It is believed that the laws of atomic and sub-atomic physics already known to us will eventually bring about an understanding also of the set of processes we call life, this being indicated by the gradual movement of the concepts of physics into the realm of molecular biology. Already, the overriding conclusion is that the whole of the physical universe – and that means you, me, the earth on which we stand, the Sun, Moon and stars – is composed purely of energy manifested in one way or another. So, when we observe a spiral, we are seeing a pattern in energy, itself made up of an infinite array of tiny spiral vortices – the spinning threads of the sub-atomic particles themselves.

Quantum physicists, including the American David Bohm (1917–92), formerly professor of theoretical physics at Birkbeck College, London, have postulated some kind of 'information' medium, or 'super-spectrum' perhaps, as the cause of things which are often described as paranormal. Somehow, such a medium may cause particles to form in space and enable particles to communicate with one another. For example, if two particles are propelled in opposite directions and a magnet placed in the path of one to alter its spin, then the other particle will also change its spin. It has been suggested that this 'news' could be carried on an electromagnetic wave which travels at the speed of light – such waves are light, but not necessarily visible light.

Bohm, who had worked with Einstein at Princeton University in the early 1950s, developed a theory of quantum physics which took a holistic view of existence, his scientific and philosophical views having become inseparable. He was a thinker who was unafraid to challenge scientific orthodoxy, his interests and influence reaching well beyond physics into the realms of biology, psychology, religion, art and the future prospects for society.

In 1959, Bohm read a book by the Indian philosopher J Krishna-murti and realised how his own ideas on quantum mechanics blended with Krishnamurti's philosophical ideas. Bohm's approach to philosophy and physics, which saw matter and consciousness as an interrelated whole, found expression in his 'Wholeness and the Implicate Order' (1980), in which he argued that the 'unbroken wholeness' of all existence could be seen as an undivided flowing movement without boundaries, and that, ultimately, it would be shown that there was no distinction between mind and matter.

'The mental and the material are two sides of one overall process that are (like form and content) separated only in thought and not in actuality,' he said. 'Rather, there is one energy that is the basis of all reality...' ('A New Theory of the Relationship of Mind and Matter', from the 'Journal of the American Society of Psychical Research', 1986, vol 80, no 2).

Bohm envisaged an 'implicate order', embracing time, space and matter, although the presence of it could be only inferred by observation of its various manifestations. This implicate order 'unfolded' into the explicate order, the visible and tangible universe. Bohm's analogy was a pattern made from small cuts in a folded piece of paper which was then unfolded. Widely separated elements of the pattern were then produced by the same original cuts in the folded paper. The cuts represented the implicate order and the unfolded pattern the explicate order.

It reminds one of the creation ideas expressed in certain mystical systems, such as the Kabbalah and Gnosticism, and even in shamanism, and it seems to me that the spiral form could be a kind of bridge between the implicate and the explicate orders, manifesting itself out of the former into the latter, from the pleroma into the physical plane.

Bohm believed that all objects and events in the visible, or explicate, world were relatively autonomous, stable, and temporary 'sub-totalities' arising from the deeper, implicate order of unbroken wholeness. In 'Wholeness and the Implicate Order', he likened this to the flow of a stream, saying: 'On this stream, one may see an ever-changing pattern of vortices, ripples, waves, splashes, etc, which evidently have no independent existence as such. Rather, they are abstracted from the flowing movement, arising and vanishing in the total process of the flow. Such transitory subsistence as may be possessed by these abstracted forms implies only a relative independence or autonomy of behaviour, rather than absolutely independent existence as ultimate substances.'

It was Bohm's hope that people would eventually recognise the fundamental inter-relatedness of all things and would join together to create a more holistic and harmonious world.

Dr June Singer, the American Jungian psychologist, in 'Seeing through the visible world' (1980), makes a comparison between Bohm and Jung. She says: 'We experience the explicate order when we perceive realities with our senses. Our familiar world is one of separate objects subject to various physical forces like gravity, etc. We can see that certain things may be in relationship to each other, and in this explicate world of things and thoughts, we can hope to integrate the various disparate parts. Wholeness appears to us as an ideal state of being... For Jung, the collective unconscious was the fundamental reality, with human consciousness deriving from it. In a similar way, Bohm sees the implicate order as the fundamental reality, with the explicate order and all its manifestations as derivative.'

When we look at spirality in nature, we see an image of creation, a pattern formed in energy – indeed, all natural energy appears to move in spirals – but what we do not see, cannot see, is that cosmic force which has manipulated that energy into the visible shape taken by matter. And here we encounter the deepest part of the mystery. You might wonder what that force could be. Is it perhaps that mysterious 'dark energy' which has today's astrophysicists so puzzled, or perhaps some other force or property associated with it? Or do we simply accept the metaphor of a divine signature, referring to the 'hand of God', do we believe that 'Nature knows best', or pay simple homage to the 'life-force'?

Just as water drains away down the plughole in a swirling spiral, channelled thus by the 'force' exerted on it by the sides of the bath, so some force must act on or within matter in a similar way to 'bend' it into the spiral curve. To give another analogy from everyday experience, as a guitarist I have often noticed how, when fitting new strings to the instrument, the leading length of a string threaded through a machine peg – which is then turned to tighten the string to pitch – will bend into a perfect equiangular spiral curve if it is caught against an adjacent peg as the string is wound on. The adjacent peg, like the sides of the bath, represents that unknown and seemingly intelligent force which creates the spiral pattern in all its universal efficacy and applicability. However, even if we were able to identify this force, how could we know how it arose, or how it was being directed – indeed, what was the 'force behind the force'? We would find ourselves in the self-defeating situation of an infinite regress.

Vladimir B Ginzburg, the Russian mechanical engineer, technical scientist and researcher in physics, who was born in Moscow and moved to the USA in 1974, theorises that the basic substance of the universe is a 'spiral field' which accounts for its infinite nature. In his books, 'Spiral Grain of the Universe' (1997) and 'Unified Spiral Field

116

and Matter' (1999), he describes in accessible story form how, since the time of Archimedes, the spiral field theory could have been proposed by a whole range of scientists and philosophers, including Descartes, Kepler, Leibniz, Swedenborg, Faraday, Ampere, Fresnel, William Thomson (Lord Kelvin), Weber, Hertz and Tait.

Ginzburg's maths is complicated, requiring an abandonment of the century-old relativistic equations derived from Einstein (although Ginzburg claims his calculations can be understood by high school students). Broadly, he sets out to prove that a spiral field propagates around all objects in the universe, and that it governs the motion of objects as well the forces exerted upon them. The spiral field is in the shape of a torus – resembling a ring doughnut – which, geometrically, is formed when a closed curve is rotated about a line which lies in the same plane but does not intersect it. His theory clearly has profound implications for particle physics as it claims to provide an explanation for, among other things, the nature of electromagnetic waves, neutrinos, the structure of elementary particles and atoms, and the complexities of nuclear reactions.

It seems to me that Ginzburg's extraordinary work – although it has to be said that the Ancient Egyptians probably got there first with their concept of *neb* – complements the ideas of Bohm (implicate order), Dawkins (memes) and Jung (archetypes/pleroma), and also the morphic resonance theory of biologist Rupert Sheldrake, which we shall be looking at in the next chapter. While, of course, Ginzburg's theory deals specifically with the spiral form, the uniting element of all these ideas seems to be the notion of some rarefied continuum, or field, or force, separate from, but impinging upon, the material universe. Each of these theorists, coming at the subject from their different disciplines, may well be in possession of a part of the truth.

HOLD FAST TO THE VOID

Certainly, the spiral conveys information to us, in all its many and varied manifestations; it also conveys information to its constituent parts and to its environment, whether it be a galaxy or a DNA molecule in the cell, establishing a code which is nature's way of using the information to decide form, or structure.

It gives a new twist to the famous dictum of Canadian media guru Marshall McLuhan (1911–80), 'the medium is the message', which suggests it is the medium itself that shapes and controls the scale and form of material association and action.

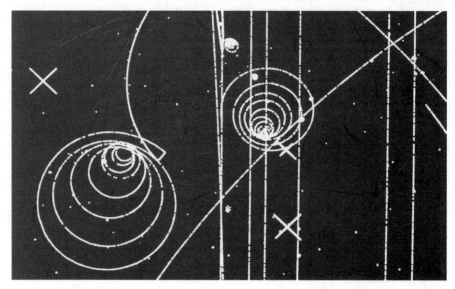

Spiral tracks of colliding sub-atomic particles in a bubble chamber.

How the spiral makes its swirling magic even among the elementary particles has been witnessed through the use of complex equipment including 'bubble chambers' in which any electrically charged particle leaves a clear track which can be photographed and analysed as it moves through a supercooled chamber filled with liquefied gas.

The particles are spiralled in on a beam from a particle accelerator, a machine which is used to increase the velocity and hence the kinetic energy of the particles or nuclei, and spiral tracks are formed as particles collide, creating other charged particles. Powerful magnetic fields cause these particles to spiral to the left or the right, according to the electric charge, and the degree of curvature of their paths gives physicists essential information about their charge, speed and mass. The pattern of electro-magnetic fields is a spiral, and when a moving electron, for example, encounters a magnetic environment it is forced to spiral along the line of the magnetic field.

Arthur Koestler (1905–83), the Hungarian-born novelist, critic and philosopher, commented on the surrealistic nature of the world which the sub-molecular physicists have created, a world which is also of great mystery and beauty, where events in the bubble chamber show 'the trajectories of unimaginably small particles moving at unimaginable speeds in curves and spirals, colliding, recoiling, or exploding and giving birth to other particles'.

The collisions of particles are the main experimental method of studying their properties and interactions, and the patterns they trace are therefore of great importance. Matter in these experiments has shown itself to be completely liable to change. All particles can be transmuted into other particles and, created from energy, they can disappear into energy.

> 'There all the barrel-hoops are knit,
> There all the serpent tails are bit,
> There all the gyres converge in one,
> There all the planets drop in the sun.'

W B Yeats (1865–1939), *Supernatural Songs*

As has been demonstrated, a motive force, or field, in the universe tends to create spirality at all levels, and in the sub-atomic realm choreographs a 'cosmic dance' involving a continuous interplay of energy patterns which, together with the theory of the oscillating universe, brings to mind the endless cycles of birth and rebirth envisaged in Eastern religion and philosophy.

The idea of a cyclic universe is of ancient origin. People have considered it from the beginning of recorded history. The ancient Hindus, for example, had a sophisticated and finely tuned cosmology founded on a cyclic universe, and the Chinese Tao, one of the oldest and most venerable philosophies concerning the universe, also embraced the idea, which has kept recurring in Western thought too: for instance, Edgar Allen Poe and Friedrich Nietzsche both supported it, and in the early days of relativity theory Albert Einstein was interested in it.

Correspondences between events in the macrocosm and in the microcosm – from cartwheeling star systems in outer space to the sub-atomic carousel of elementary particles in inner space – suggest a definable pattern of movement throughout the cosmos governed by an eternal law of change, obviously unaffected even by the death and rebirth of universes. Change appears as the only constant amid the myriad combinations and transformations of minds and matter which, to the eye of limited vision, register only a meaningless chaos.

> 'There is no constant existence, neither of our being, nor of the objects. And we, and our judgement, and all mortall things else, do uncessantly rowle, turne, and passe away.'

Michel Eyquem de Montaigne (1533–92),
An Apologie of Raymond Sebond, 1576

'Since 'tis Nature's law to change,
Constancy alone is strange.'

John Wilmot, Earl of Rochester (1647–80)

The Chinese Tao refers essentially to the totality of the natural process, cosmic and human. The Tao, or the Way, is cyclic; it is the principle of the universe which generates all things, and is the source and way of creation, narrowly transcribed into English as 'God'. It represents the right way, the way of heaven and of humanity, an ideal state of complete harmony between Earth and Heaven. Central to Chinese consciousness for perhaps 5,000 years has been the recognition of the masculine and feminine principles, yin and yang, and in the beginning this primal polarity sprang from the Tao. Yang was the original act of creation of the universe, and yin the steadying factor which permitted order to arise out of original chaos. Yang equates with Heaven, and yin with Earth.

The Chinese expression to describe yin and yang together is *qi*, meaning the energy or life force from which everything else emerges. And in the familiar symbol, the 'Diagram of the Supreme Ultimate', signifying the relationship between yin and yang and the Way, what do we find but the spiral curve once again, there in the line which bonds the two archetypal polarities together, emphasising their symmetry and inter-dependence, and indicating a continuous cyclic movement or flow. The two dots in the diagram encapsulate the idea that each time one of the forces reaches its extreme, it already contains in itself the seed of its opposite.

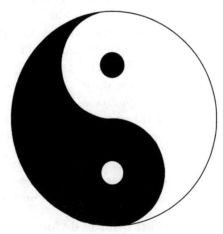

The Yin Yang symbol.

120

'The vacuum is truly a "living Void", pulsating in endless rhythms of creation and destruction. The discovery of the dynamic quality of the vacuum is seen by many physicists as one of the most important findings of modern physics. From its role as an empty container of the physical phenomena, the void has emerged as a dynamic quantity of utmost importance.'

Fritjof Capra (1939–), *The Tao of Physics*, 1975

Clearly, there are parallels between Eastern mysticism and modern physics, which sees form and space as part of a single continuum called the quantum field. The laws of quantum physics state that particles are constantly being created out of nothing and annihilated. This means that even an apparently empty vacuum has a non–zero potential energy. If our universe could be created by such 'vacuum fluctuation' then so could others.

Today, the vacuum is regarded as the most complex aspect of the universe because it embraces all particles and all forces, including those which are as yet unknown to science. The idea arises from one of the basic tenets of quantum physics, the Heisenberg uncertainty principle, named after the German physicist Werner Heisenberg (1901–76) who pioneered the mathematics of the sub-atomic realm during the 1920s. His theory of quantum mechanics was published in 1925 when he was only 23. For this theory and the applications of it, which also resulted in the discovery of allotropic forms of hydrogen, he was awarded the Nobel Prize for physics for 1932.

Put simply, his discovery was that the more you know of a particle's momentum, the less you can know about its position, and vice versa. As you acquire knowledge of one property, so you lose knowledge of the other; the more you find out how much energy a particle has, the less you know about when it has that energy. Therefore, the determination of the position and momentum of a particle in motion necessarily contains errors and, although such errors are negligible on the human scale, they cannot be ignored in studies of the quantum world. The odd upshot of all this is that these relationships fill the vacuum with an infinitude of evanescent particles which flicker in and out of existence.

Scientists now think that the vacuum holds the key to an understanding of the mysterious antigravity force that pushes the galaxies away from each other and also flattens out the universe, giving space the minimum curvature, rather as a shrivelled balloon is made

121

smooth as it is inflated and, as it gets larger, its surface appears more and more flat.

If this 'dark energy' does come to be understood, then the physics that drove the Big Bang will be understood also, along with that of the crucial period which came immediately after – the inflationary period, referred to above. The suggestion is that, due to all the sub-atomic particles constantly blinking in and out of existence, the vacuum had a kind of pressure which built up to an enormous level, suddenly causing it to expand in all directions, inflating the fabric of space-time with incredible power and speed.

The concept of *qi* – the constant process of creation and disintegration – seems to represent an intuitive understanding of this new view of the vacuum long before the West became scientifically equipped to observe the phenomenon and realise that, like the Eastern void, space is not a state of simple nothingness, but contains the potentiality, the energy, for all forms of the particle world which make up all of matter. These forces, however, are not independent physical entities but merely transient manifestations of the underlying void.

It seems that the human mind has never been prepared to accept that space on a universal scale is empty and pointless. Epicurus (c341–271BC) suggested that there was a 'principle of plenitude' in nature, an eternal fount of being, the implication being that there will always be fulfilment of any potentiality, ensuring that the universe will continue to produce life, simply because it can.

Epicurus, who studied philosophy under followers of Democritus and Plato, and who, in Athens, founded the Garden, a combination of philosophical community and school, taught that the basic constituents of the world are the atoms, irreducible pieces of matter whirling through space, and he tried to explain all natural phenomena in atomic terms. His materialistic metaphysics rejected the existence of Platonic Forms and an immaterial soul, and he said that the gods had no influence on our lives.

Again, in this chapter, macrocosm is reflected in microcosm, 'as above, so below', and vice versa, and the spiral as the indicator of the network of vortices of time and change which is called the Tao, the cease-less inflow and outflow of the creative, universal energy which makes and sustains all things, which transforms interstellar gas and dust into planets where inanimate atoms can be metamorphosed into intelligent life. And the elements that compose the body of the Earth and of human beings are plentiful throughout the cosmos and life, it is thought, could appear on any planet with a suitable climate.

So the spiral now stands not only for the cyclic law of birth, growth, decay and death and rebirth, but also for the hope for life elsewhere in the universe. Spirality equals reality.

'Is not the space between heaven and earth like a bellows?
It is empty without being exhausted:
The more it works the more comes out.
Much speech leads inevitably to silence.
Better to hold fast to the void.'

Lao Tzu, *Tao Te Ching*, c500BC

6

Coil of Life

'O spiral of ascension
From the vultured urn
Of the morning
Of man when
The land
And
The
Born sea
Praised the sun...'

Dylan Thomas, *Vision and Prayer*

About four billion years ago, a billion years after the Earth was formed, atoms in the atmosphere were fused together, perhaps by electrical discharge from lightning, into molecules of amino acids and small units known as nucleotides, which constitute the foundations of living matter. These eventually drained into the great primeval ocean where, at this dawn of creation, the sublime powers of the spiral again came to galvanise matter into coherence, this time to identify itself inextricably with life in the double helix of the DNA molecule.

Every organism that there is now on the Earth has tiny coils called chromosomes which contain DNA (deoxyribonucleic acid), the carrier of the hereditary message from one generation to another. The molecule is made up of nucleotides, and it is these which actually determine the genetic code. All life-forms share the code – a strong indication that all life on Earth originated in a single forebear, back in that organic 'soup' in the seas of the young planet.

'Form is the physical equivalent of memory... memory is the mind's embodiment of form.'

Norman Mailer (1923–), *Cannibals and Christians*, 1966

'Form is the shaping force in life.'

Lyall Watson (1939–),
Lifetide: a biology of the unconscious, 1979

Now, the idea of form as an evolutionary conditioner goes back to the Ancient Greeks: Aristotle (384–322BC) – pre-dating Norman Mailer by more than 2,000 years – said that mind was a function of form and shape, suggesting that substance was able to receive an idea and assume a form capable of fulfilling a function. Aristotle, who was born at Stagirus, a Greek colony and seaport on the coast of Thrace, was sent to Athens at the age of 17 to study at the Academy under Plato, where he remained for 20 years. But whereas Plato located ultimate reality in Ideas or eternal Forms, knowable only through contemplation and reason, Aristotle saw ultimate reality in physical objects, knowable through experience.

Nuclear physics bears out Aristotle's view on form in its belief, touched upon above, that matter is a form of energy. The South African-born biologist and anthropologist Lyall Watson, who gained his doctor of philosophy degree under the supervision of Desmond Morris at London Zoo, said molecular biology showed that the biological consequences of matter were dictated directly by the shape or form of living things: 'The real transition from non–living to living matter was made with the impression on simple organic substances of an essential shape, that of the famous double helix of DNA.'

Genes, which are made of DNA, themselves make more DNA and specify, via RNA (ribonucleic acid), the construction of vital proteins which are the agents that carry out the processes of life. DNA makes RNA which, in a spiral unit, itself makes protein which makes more DNA possible.

It has been demonstrated that all forms of life grow according to the code contained in the DNA helix. It replicates cell construction, structuring the organism to resemble its parents perfectly with the inherited characteristics of both, handed down in the genes from the mother and father. The double helix of the human DNA molecule has the shape of a coiling ladder, with its rungs comprising four chemical bases: adenine, thymine, cytosine and guanine.

Helices are formed by two extremely lengthy sugar and phosphate chain molecules (the sides of the 'ladder') which wind around one another. The 'rungs' of the ladder are formed by the base molecules which jut out from the two chains, pointing towards each other in pairs, and which link up through the action of weak chemical bonds.

For making proteins – the molecules of living matter – the genes, which decide the species to which an organism will belong, together with most of its individual characteristics, are contained in this series of hydrogen-based chemical links between the two interweaving strands of DNA. The sequence of these links, which may be likened to the steps on a spiral staircase, determines the order in which protein sub-units are assembled and therefore the kind of protein it is. The complete 'staircase', which is divided into 24 units of unequal length corresponding to as many different chromosomes, has about three billion rungs.

A representation of the DNA double helix.

The protein-creating process starts when the intertwined DNA strands 'unzip' and the unpaired links find new partners from among the stock of spare molecules to build up a mirror image of the sequence, which is the 'messenger' RNA. When this 'unzips', the pairing process is repeated, only this time the connections are made in threes, and attached to each new chemical link by another variety of RNA coil ('transfer' RNA) is an amino acid or protein sub-unit, the fundamental building block of an organism.

Here lies the hidden secret of life, in the spiral code of DNA. Intriguingly, early research into DNA and RNA, which took place in the late 1930s, was in the Stockholm laboratories of the Swedish cytologist and geneticist Torbjorn Caspersson (1910–97) who developed a system combining spectroscope and quartz-lensed microscope which could locate precisely the nucleic acids in different parts of an individual living cell. Quartz is formed by molecules of silicon dioxide coming together in a spiral or helicoid shape: like seeking like!

In his book 'The Double Helix', the zoologist James Watson, one of the participants in the discovery in the early 1950s of the DNA structure, describes how his pulse began to race as he suddenly realised its 'profound implications'. The existence of two intertwined chains could not be a chance matter but strongly suggested that one chain in each molecule had at some earlier stage served as the template for the syntheses of the other chain. Under such a scheme, gene replication began with the separation of two identical chains. Then two new daughter strands were made on the two parental templates, thereby creating two DNA molecules identical to the original molecule.

Chicago-born Watson joined the Cavendish laboratories at Cambridge at a time when Francis Crick, Maurice Wilkins, Rosalind Franklin and Linus Pauling were racing to determine the structure of DNA. X-ray crystallography experiments by Franklin and Wilkins elicited much information about DNA – in particular that it was a molecule in which two 'strands' formed a tightly linked pair. Crick and Watson made the intuitive leap. In 1953, they proposed that the structure of DNA was a winding helix in which pairs of bases (adenine with thymine and guanine with cytosine) held the two strands together. The Watson–Crick model of the DNA double helix provided enormous impetus for research in the emerging fields of molecular genetics and biochemistry, and Watson, Crick and Wilkins were awarded the Nobel Prize in 1962.

Watson – a man known to leave his shoes untied due to absent-mindedness – went on to teach at Harvard and CalTech, and from 1968 was director of Cold Spring Harbor Laboratory in New York which became one of the world's leading research centres for molecular biology. Watson, who famously said 'I think people are born curious and have it pounded out of them', has made major contributions to the understanding of the genetic code, including being involved in the finding that DNA molecules do not merely reproduce themselves, but also produce templates for the mass production of all the other chemical ingredients of life.

Proteins make up 18 per cent of the weight of the human body, and one further appreciates the fundamental significance of DNA when, for example, it is realised that respiratory carriers, such as haemoglobin, are protein molecules. So too are the antibodies that match and neutralise hundreds of thousands of substances which the body may recognise as foreign. Enzymes are protein molecules which enable cells to make energy, other enzymes, more DNA, and new cells.

The chromosomes themselves, where the genetic code is stored in the sequence of chemical links, are made of protein and DNA bound inseparably together. Every protein molecule, moreover, has a 'backbone' of basic amino acids which coils into a helix – the 'alpha helix' as it is known.

In many parts of the body, the alpha helix causes fibrous tissues to coil in the same way. Collagen fibres, for example, which contain the chief constituent of the threads of connecting tissue (as in skin and tendon) and of the organic substances of the bones, are regarded as having a molecule comprising three alpha helices wrapped together. These triple helices twist together to form larger and larger coils until a helical fibre is made which is big enough, and strong enough, to be seen with an everyday microscope. All these helices, like those of DNA molecules, are right-handed – continually turning away from chaos and towards order.

So it was the evolution of the nucleic acids – those 'blueprints' in which the secret of life lies guarded by the windings of the DNA labyrinth – in the 'primeval soup' billions of years ago, which prepared the way for the development of living cells within each of which DNA orchestrates the activities of countless molecules in such a configuration, even, that part of their number forms a protective shield about the rest.

The American research scholar and historian of science Horace Freeland Judson, in his impressive book 'The Eighth Day of Creation', a complete historical account of the central line of discoveries in molecular biology, said that after its discovery, DNA, the master substance in the cell, 'turned out to be a substance of elegance, even beauty ... functions are united in DNA with such ingenious parsimony that one smiles with the delight of perceiving it'.

The earliest forms of life were so simple that there was little to distinguish them from the lifeless molecules which came before. Somehow – and no one knows exactly how because no record remains – the cell evolved, and then a control centre in the cell where the DNA came to be located, allowing greater proliferation of cells. These living cells split into two kinds, first one with the properties of a plant, and then one with those of an animal. The extension of the jurisdiction of the DNA molecule beyond the boundaries of a single cell made possible the organisation of cells into bodies.

However, the latest thinking among evolutionary biologists is that DNA had a forerunner of some kind. The question has been raised because DNA is unable to replicate without a large number of accompanying molecules, including proteins that can be made only by

DNA-coded information, creating a potential chicken-and-egg situation. A number of scientists now think that RNA may have been the original replicator, and have propounded the 'RNA World' theory. The idea is that, before proteins existed, RNA could have acted as its own catalyst. Without a partner chain with which to pair in a double helix structure such as that of DNA, RNA is able to pair with parts of itself, either making a miniature double helix, or another shape.

The conclusion is that RNA has some of the replicator virtues of DNA as well as some of the enzyme virtues of proteins – enzymes being substances which act as a catalyst to promote a specific biochemical reaction. Perhaps, before becoming DNA, the 'arch-replicator', and before the existence of proteins, there was a time when RNA alone had enough of both virtues to stand in for both. As it is known that RNA can catalyse reactions elsewhere, it is thought possible that it could have catalysed its own synthesis. After all, it is also known that DNA is good at replicating, while being bad at being an enzyme.

'Perhaps an RNA fire ignited itself in the original world,' says Professor Richard Dawkins in 'The Ancestor's Tale' (2004), 'And then later started to make proteins that turned around and helped synthesise RNA, and later DNA too, which took over as the dominant replicator.'

He adds: 'If we accept the RNA World theory, there would have been a major transition or watershed, when a world of RNA serving as both replicator and enzyme gave over to a separation between DNA in the replicator role and proteins in the enzyme role. Then there was the clubbing together of replicating entities (genes) in cells with walls, which prevented the gene products leaking away and kept them together with the products of other genes with which they could collaborate in cellular chemistry.'

Just as the ability of DNA to control other molecules permitted the evolution of the cell, so the subsequent improvement of the chemical messenger system, whereby the DNA molecules in one cell could be answerable to those in another, allowed the development of multi-cellular organisms. The plant cells produced oxygen as a waste product which the animal cells were able to absorb, leading directly to the evolution of intelligent life.

It was more than another three billion years of evolution, however, before the first animals with external skeletons emerged – molluscs and snails, for example, with their shells spirally shaped for extra protection – and almost four billion years, from fish to amphibian to reptile to mammal, before humans appeared and their own special kind of consciousness developed.

Genome is the name given to the complete set of genetic material of an organism, a kind of code which transmits the form of the molecular make-up of the body from generation to generation; the act of giving form to the atoms that serve as the raw material is known as gene expression. The most amazing property of the genome is its very meaning. It is simply the narrator of the story of life.

Michael Hayes sees a natural harmony arising from DNA and the genetic code which he has found reflected in all the major religions and esoteric traditions which have embraced it as a code of conduct, 'a harmonious mode of being', founded on the principles of musical and *pi* symmetry – the same symmetry evident in the structure of DNA.

'Nature's evolutionary processes,' he says, 'Encoded within the musical structure of DNA and the genetic code, continue to evolve higher still, beyond the confines of the physical brain encased in the skull, into scales of existence that ultimately encompass the entire universe.' He sees DNA as the fundamental manifestation of the Hermetic Code, by which all evolution has proceeded, from the lowest life form to human consciousness.

Dr Rupert Sheldrake, the British biochemist and biologist (whose wife is Jill Purce, the author of 'The Mystic Spiral' mentioned in my third chapter), believes that a formative principle in nature drives living processes. He has brought the idea of 'morphic resonance' to the study of naturally occurring patterns. He supports the proposal first made by the Russian scientist Alexander Gurwitsch in 1922 that 'morphogenetic fields' give rise to form – morphogenesis being the process under which all biological forms develop from simpler forms. These fields are said to govern cells and tissues by arranging their characteristic shapes in the embryo.

For Sheldrake, author of 'A New Science of Life' (1981), DNA alone is not enough to explain morphogenesis. This is because, if part of an embryo is removed, the remaining section still has a morphogenetic field associated with it. The field is continuous and holistic, not atomistic, and so bits cannot be cut away from them; the complete form is restored because the field remains whole. As Sheldrake says, this 'brings more from less'.

He thinks that, over time, morphogenetic fields could be the cause of what happens to any given species, which would mean that the species is influenced by, and remains connected to, all of its past manifestations. This is what he means by 'morphic resonance' which, fundamentally, is a holistic concept of natural form and growth, although conventional science has yet to catch up with this notion, still being

130

rooted in mechanistic and reductionist approaches. David Bohm, of course, similarly set a challenge for the reductionist outlook with his holistic concept of the implicate order. 'The nature of creativity is really a philosophical question which does not lie within the realm of natural sciences,' Sheldrake says.

His hypothesis of formative causation predicts, for example, that as animals of a given species learn a new pattern of behaviour, other similar animals will subsequently tend to learn the same thing more readily all over the world; the more that learn it, the easier it should become for others. He suggests that morphic resonance is responsible for the way in which patterns and forms are repeated in nature, although his theory does not explain how the first particular forms or patterns originated.

I would venture to say that their provenance lies in the kind of implicate order envisaged by Bohm, and that we detect the resonance – the 'sculpting' of random energy into pattern and form – in the explicate order, the world of things.

As the energy, the chemical elements, which make up the Earth and all life upon it, burst from the hearts of exploding stars which, aeons ago, were themselves wrought in the matrix of the ur-spiral, the human mind must have been resonant with the immanent imprint from the earliest times. Out of the implicate and into the explicate!

Morphic resonance theory now seems to be supported, or certainly complemented, by the new science of epigenetics which suggests that the environment and lived experiences can not only modify genes but that such modifications can be inherited – harking back to the long-decried 19th century Lamarckian theory of evolution which proposed that 'acquired characteristics' could be handed down from generation to generation.

Epigenetics involves the idea that genes can 'remember' events, and that the memory is inherited; it is the study of how information can be passed from a cell to its descendants without it being strictly encoded in the DNA sequence. Instead, the gene can be altered in other ways, and studies are already providing evidence of epigenetic inheritance in humans. The major upshot of this is that evolution could be seen as capable of responding to artificial stimuli, which goes completely against the thinking of conventional genetics.

Fascinatingly, Sheldrake has also set out ideas for amplifying Jung's concept of the collective unconscious and archetypal psychology in a two-part paper 'Mind, memory and archetype: morphic resonance and the collective unconscious' and 'Society, spirit and ritual: morphic resonance and the collective unconscious' (Psychic Perspectives, spring and autumn, 1987).

Applying his morphic resonance theory to memory, Sheldrake says he believes we tune into other people's memories as well as our own. He suggests there is a collective memory which forms a background against which our own experience and individual memories develop, a concept much akin to that of Jung's.

Taking the example of rituals, Sheldrake says they have a kind of deliberate and conscious evocation of memory, all the way back to the first act: 'If morphic resonance occurs as I think it does, (the) conservatism of ritual would create exactly the right conditions for morphic resonance to occur between those performing the ritual now and all those who performed it previously. The ritualised commemorations and participatory re-linking with the ancestors of all cultures might involve just that; it might, in fact, be literally true that these rituals enable the current participants to reconnect with their ancestors (in some sense) through morphic resonance.'

Jung's idea was applied primarily to human experience and human collective memory, but Sheldrake goes further to suggest that a similar principle operates throughout the entire universe, not just in human beings. 'If the kind of radical paradigm shift I am talking about goes on within biology – if the hypothesis of morphic resonance is even approximately correct – then Jung's idea of the collective unconscious would become a mainstream idea,' Sheldrake says. 'Morphogenic fields and the concept of the collective unconscious would completely change the context of modern psychology.'

Indeed, and if that happened, morphic resonance theory would have led to a radical reaffirmation of the concept of the collective unconscious. And it needs reaffirmation, Sheldrake asserts, because the current mechanistic context of conventional biology, medicine and psychology denies that there can be any such thing as the collective unconscious; the concept of a collective memory of a race or species has been excluded as even a theoretical possibility.

'You cannot have any inheritance of acquired characteristics according to conventional theory; you can only have an inheritance of genetic mutations,' he says. 'Under the premises of conventional biology, there would be no way that the experiences and myths of, for example, African tribes, would have any influence on the dreams of someone in Switzerland of non-African descent, which is the sort of thing Jung thought did happen.'

If we regard the spiral, and the rituals which have been associated with it over millennia, as archetypal patterns, as I suggested in chapter two – remembering that Jung says the unconscious is made up of archetypes – then morphic resonance theory, and epigenetics, could endorse the role of the collective unconscious in providing an explanation for the repetition of these forms throughout the history of human culture.

THE MYTH OF CONSCIOUSNESS

@ **'We are descended from reptiles and mammals both. In the daytime repression of the R-complex and in the night-time stirring of the dream dragons we may each of us be re-playing the hundred-million-year-old warfare between the reptiles and the mammals.'**

Carl Sagan (1934–96), *The Dragons of Eden*, 1989

A marked leap forward in the growth of the human brain, the ultimate (so far) goal of DNA's evolutionary thrust, began about a million years ago. It may be that the onset of a series of ice ages, and the necessary survival skills which human beings had to acquire as a result, led to the rapid development of the brain, which can be seen as comprising three distinct parts, each representing a separate evolutionary step.

Most ancient of these parts of the brain is the reptilian or 'R-complex' which probably evolved several hundred million years ago and which man shares with other mammals and reptiles. Surrounding the R-complex is the limbic system which, probably evolving more than 140 million years ago, is found in other mammals but not in full in reptiles; and over-topping that, the neocortex, the most recent and sudden development (between 500,000 years ago and today), which is particularly characteristic of man. Humans evolved more in this latter period than in the previous three million years.

The neurologist Paul MacLean, a prominent American researcher into brain evolution, is an advocate of 'microgenesis', which is the name given to the idea that the structure of the brain reflects its evolution over millennia. The three brains – the 'triune' brain – are like the layers of an archaeological site, each corresponding to a different stage of evolution, each connected to the others, but each operating individually with its own 'personality'. The beauty of the MacLean paradigm is that it separates out instinctual, emotional and rational behaviour, and provides an explanation as to how the brain developed over time and for what purposes, and how the three levels coexist and complement each other.

MacLean says the three brains operate like 'three interconnected biological computers, (each) with its own special intelligence, its own subjectivity, its own sense of time and space and its own memory'. He suggests that the R-complex (his term) plays a major role in ritualistic and hierarchical behaviour, as well as in aggression and territoriality, and does in fact represent a reptilian component of human nature. It may be valid here to suggest a link with the spiritually revitalising rituals of geomancers which were enacted to invoke what they described as the dragon currents of the Earth.

Containing the 'labyrinth of the mind', the head is the inner sanctum of the temple of man's body, both originated and guarded by the windings of that labyrinth. With each turn, the brain completed a stage in its evolution, the number of 'gyres', or folds, in the cerebrum being at its greatest in humans to facilitate higher mental processes, and to control thought and consciousness, through its large surface area. Indian thought has traditionally identified both the mind and the natural appearance of the brain with the winding paths of the labyrinth.

Various esoteric spiritual traditions have envisaged three planes of consciousness and even three different brains. George Gurdjieff (c1866–1949), the Armenian-born mystic and charismatic, referred to man as a 'three-brained being', one for the spirit, one for the soul, and one for the body. Similar ideas can be found in the Kabbalah and in Platonism, with the association of spirit and head (the brain itself), soul and heart, and body and belly. There is also the sequence of the *chakras*, with points along the body or the spine which correspond to levels of consciousness in an ascending manner, from gross to subtle.

Itzhak Bentov, the Czechoslovakian thinker who moved to America where he became an innovator in the field of medical instruments and bio-medical engineering, but where he died in a plane crash in 1979, offered a new perspective on human consciousness and its possibilities. He suggested that consciousness is the common uniting element of all creation, and that through this link all things are in constant contact. His is a holistic model of the universe that encompasses not only the physical, observable objects that make up our immediate environment but also the distant universe and other 'realities'.

According to Bentov, consciousness evolves to the 'absolute' which is the source of all consciousness. Matter, composed of quanta of energy, is the vibrating, changing component of pure consciousness. The absolute is fixed, manifest and invisible. Ours, then, is a vibratory reality, from microcosm to macrocosm. Realities are relative, depending on the position and condition of the observer. We all know the everyday human reality, but most of us do not know that our consciousness can be schooled to expand and interact with the whole spectrum of realities which are, in fact, different states of consciousness. The goal of creation is the evolution of consciousness to higher levels, says Bentov, and the opposing forces of good and evil are there to encourage this evolution.

Following Bentov's approach, spirality would have to be a direct product of consciousness in the universe, as well as being the self-promoting symbol of consciousness, and of that latent creative consciousness waiting to be endowed.

More recently, the American physicist Danah Zohar, in 'The Quantum Self' (1990), says that quantum physics holds out the promise of a new world-view, one which, like Bentov's, would give a physical basis for the more holistic, less fragmented, way of looking at ourselves. Zohar, who now lives at Oxford with her British psychiatrist husband Ian Marshall, studied physics and philosophy at MIT, and undertook her postgraduate work in philosophy, religion and psychology at Harvard University. She believes that consciousness is the bridge between the classical world and the quantum world.

In investigating the nature of individual identity and its relationship to the universe at large, she and Marshall conclude that human beings, as in the sub-atomic realm, show the same wave and particle duality described by Heisenberg's uncertainty principle. Our perceived individuality, our sense of being separate from others, is equivalent to the behaviour of a sub-atomic particle while the way we inter-relate with others, and the world, is more in the manner of a wave. If we look at people from the quantum perspective both these aspects appear. She says the quantum self is simply a more fluid self, changing and evolving at each moment, now separating into sub-selves, now reuniting in a larger self, but always in some way being itself.

Zohar says: 'Once we have seen that the physics of human consciousness emerge from quantum processes within the brain and that in consequence human consciousness and the whole world of its creation shares a physics with everything else in the universe... it becomes impossible to imagine a single aspect of our lives that is not drawn into one coherent whole.'

The basic building blocks of mind (bosons) and those of matter (fermions) arise from a common quantum substrate, the so-called vacuum, and the physics of consciousness which gives rise to the world of culture – art, ideas, values, even religion – is the same physics that creates the world of nature. Thus quantum theory brings the realisation that all sentient beings on our planet are ultimately connected and are taking part in a common destiny.

The quantum world-view affords an optimistic notion of the human self which is 'free and responsible, responsive to others and to its environment, essentially related and naturally committed, and at every moment creative'.

Moreover, the universe has an innate tendency towards life and consciousness which, ultimately, are due to the mathematical properties and behaviour of the quantum wave function, which itself favours the evolution of life and consciousness. Marshall thinks we 'must' exist and think, in accordance with the anthropic principle – that things are the way they are because otherwise we would not exist. If one accepts this – and personally, I find it a very persuasive argument – then it follows that life is indeed pure potentiality, and so can never be used up, the developmental movement of the spiral signifying this idea perfectly. And any cosmological theory must therefore embrace the fact that the universe has evolved to include us.

Psychologists, philosophers and neuroscientists still argue over the origin and function of consciousness, but it becomes much less of 'the last great mystery of science' once one accepts that it has enabled human beings to become the only creatures on the planet capable of contemplating their own existence, and has made them the very sensorium, the eyes and ears, of the universe. It is consciousness which gives the world meaning.

This idea, of course, goes back to Jung, and his 'myth of consciousness'. The cognising and reflecting consciousness gives rise to creative activity which superimposes on the existence of the outer and inner worlds, or realities, the assertion that they are *known*. For Jung, the cosmic meaning of consciousness was that man was indispensable for the completion of creation, that man himself was the 'second creator of the world', and had alone given the world its objective existence. 'Human consciousness created objective existence and meaning, and man found his indispensable place in the great process of being,' he said, in his autobiographical 'Memories, Dreams, Reflections' (1963).

The metaphysical task of human beings rests in an ongoing expansion of consciousness, and their destinies in the creation of individual self-awareness. Much of the trouble in the world today lies in the level of unconsciousness among people, and the lack of insight into themselves. I would contend that the emblem of our metaphysical task is the spiral, and that it is of great value for us to view reality, by means of the imagination, in a mythopoeic and symbolic way. He who looks inside wakes, Jung said.

Certainly, the thinking in the 'new science', touched upon in this and the previous chapter, have profound implications for the way in which we view ourselves, our planet and the universe beyond. Indeed, physics, together with biotechnology and computer science, have become the paradigmatic sciences of our time, more so than astronomy, with its contemplative aspects, or traditional biology, with its emphasis on taxonomy and measure, although the danger is that with this particular ascendancy, a view of nature as merely quantifiable and subject to mathematical rationalisation can arise, eradicating our emotional response to it.

Yet more and more we can begin to understand that, as the shamans and the ancient adepts of magic knew intuitively, everything in the universe is connected, that it is not composed largely of dead matter but that it is actually alive and replete with meaning, that completely separate and individual identity is ultimately an illusion, and that what we deem to be our personal and individual consciousness is more likely to turn out to be simply a portal to a universal consciousness. To contemplate this is an important new step in the all-important consciousness-raising process.

7

Vortex of Time

Earth's orbit is not a circle around the Sun, nor even an ellipse, but a helix. This is because the Sun, just like myriad other stars, is moving through space in an orbit of its own, together with its entire family of planets. This proper motion is the outcome of two component forces: the general rotation of our galaxy, and the Sun's motion with respect to neighbouring stars.

The latter movement occurs obliquely to the plane of the solar system, and since the Sun is moving while the Earth goes round it, the Earth actually takes a helical path in space, rather like a giant corkscrew about 186 million miles in diameter, and with a 'pitch' of about 590 million miles, the length of the Earth's annual journey with the Sun.

Meanwhile, the solar wind, which is the expansion of the Sun's corona into interplanetary space, and comprises electrons, protons, helium nuclei and other ionised material, is propelled through the solar system in an enormous spiral due to the Sun's rotation – rather like a jet of water leaving the nozzle of a lawn sprinkler.

When the spiral intersects the Earth's orbit, interactions between the solar nuclei and particles in the upper atmosphere can cause aurorae, electrical disturbances, and even communication blackouts and compass failures. The effects of the solar wind are lessened by the Earth's magnetic field, which serves to partially deflect it, and by the inner lining of the magnetic envelope which is known as the Van Allen belt. It is above the poles, where there are holes in this lining, that the aurorae, or Northern and Southern Lights, appear when the Sun is active.

Careful measurements have established beyond doubt that the Sun is travelling in the general direction of the constellation Lyra, towards a point not far from the first magnitude star Vega. As the planets circumambulate the Sun on this interstellar journey, so the Sun, oscillating back and forth through the galactic plane, circumambulates the centre of the Milky Way galaxy, affording us a macrocosmic symbol for the actualisation of the central Self in the psyche.

But there is another grand progression of events affecting human history: the precession of the equinoxes which gives rise to the Great Zodiacal Year.

We need to look at some basic Earth science here. The Earth's axis is inclined at an angle of 23 degrees 27 minutes to the perpendicular to the plane of the orbit, or 66 degrees 33 minutes to the orbital plane itself. Due to this inclination, a given point on the Earth's surface receives the Sun's light at different angles through the year, resulting in the changing seasons and the unequal lengths of day and night for a given latitude. Meanwhile, the inclination of the axis undergoes a slight change owing to a combination of various movements with various periods and magnitudes, including the Sun's own orbit around that far-off point in the Milky Way galaxy.

These movements make the Earth's axis describe a cone with the point at the centre of the planet, and this cone traces on the celestial sphere a circle 23 degrees and 27 minutes in radius around the pole of the ecliptic, or the point in the sky which represents the vertical to the centre of the orbital plane. Actually, bearing in mind the opening words of this chapter, it is not a circle, but a spiral, as the Earth moves through space with the Sun. This 'wobbling' axial movement of the Earth is similar to that of a spinning top when it balances in such a way that it describes a cone the point of which coincides with that of the top. The comparison is not completely valid because whereas the top balances on its point as it spins, the Earth has its point at the centre, creating, in fact, two cones meeting point to point.

This precessional, or 'circular', movement is the result of the Earth's shape which is not a perfect sphere but flattened at the poles and slightly

The spiral movements of the Sun and planets through space towards the star Vega in the constellation of lyra.

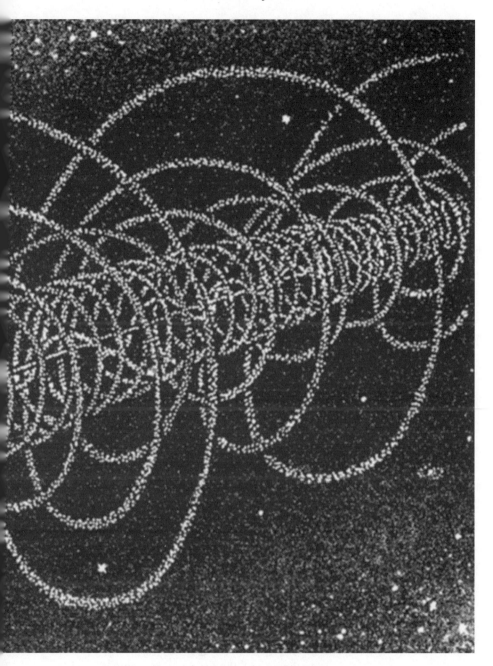

bulging at the equator. The Sun, Moon and planets, which are all more or less in the same plane, pull on the equatorial bulge, but this pull is resisted by the energy of the Earth's rotation. The Earth's axis, therefore, is caused to turn round in space. But the movement is extremely slow: the time taken by the Earth's axis to trace out one cone is about 26,000 years.

Now to explain why the movement is called the precession of the equinoxes. We must refer here to the angle between the plane of the Earth's equator and the plane of the ecliptic, which is called the obliquity of the ecliptic. The two opposite points which mark the intersection of these planes on the celestial sphere are called the equinoxes, and the Sun crosses each of them once a year. As a result of the conical movement of the Earth's axis, the plane of the equator, which is at right angles to the latter, shares the same precessional motion, but in the opposite direction to the way in which the Earth revolves.

So, as the poles describe their circles, or rather helices, on the sky, the equinoxes appear to regress with respect to the stars, hence the precession of the equinoxes, which, regressed from year to year, are finally retarded once in 2,160 years by a complete zodiacal house. Envisage then, the earth's three movements: axial, giving the 24-hour day, orbital, giving the 365-day year, and precessional, measuring the 26,000-year period which is known as the Great Year, or Platonic Year, as Plato evidently was aware of the phenomenon (see Appendix 2).

'Significantly, there are spirals, helices, literally everywhere, in all potential solar systems, in all galaxies. In the case of our own solar system, we see the planets encircling the sun, but as the entire system is perpetually moving at great velocity through space, the path traced by each planet is, in fact, a spiral. Similarly, most galaxies are spiral galaxies, which is meaningful in itself, but even so-called elliptical and irregular galaxies all revolve around a galactic centre – maybe a black hole – and all of them are hurtling across the universe at tremendous speeds, so the trajectory traced through space–time by every star is a true spiral, a helix. Furthermore, as we sit, walk or even sleep on the surface of the Earth, we are actually tracing spirals through space . . . '

Michael Hayes, *High Priests, Quantum Genes: science, religion and the theory of everything*, 2004

From the point of view of the Earth, the Sun appears to move through the constellations of the zodiac in the familiar direction: Aries,

Taurus, Gemini, Cancer, Leo, Virgo, Libra, Scorpio, Sagittarius, Capricorn, Aquarius, Pisces, from the first to the twelfth house. But from the point of view of the precession of the equinoxes, the Sun appears to move in the opposite direction, starting with Pisces and finishing with Aries.

Obviously, in our daily lives we are quite unaware of the solar system's movement through space and the mechanisms that account for the precession of the equinoxes, but they forge the image on which this chapter will be based as we return to consider the interrelated patterns of archetypes, and of synchronicity, which seem to course irresistibly through human existence, and through our individual lifetimes, in spirals.

Our images and ideas about the mysteries of existence are caught in the timeless patterns which are arrayed by the archetypes in the unconscious. In each culture and epoch, we re-create new forms for the expression of these ancient truths.

Jung's theory of synchronicity is now famous. He used the term to describe events that seemed to be connected by time and meaning, but not by cause and effect. Such 'meaningful coincidences' have no 'normal' or physical causes and so it has been conjectured that their causes are paranormal. In particular, Jung argued that these coincidences tend to occur during those emotionally charged events which he termed 'archetypal'.

Certainly, Jung's theories in this and other areas have made him to psychology what Einstein has been to physics, and indeed, it was quite early in Jung's life that he formulated the theory of synchronicity after a meeting with Einstein in Zurich at which they discussed space and time. The synchronicity theories of Jung, the Austrian biologist Paul Kammerer (1880–1926), and the Nobel Prize-winning Austrian physicist Wolfgang Pauli (1900–58), all point to a strange force in the universe seeking to bring some kind of order out of randomness, a force which, I suggest, is again represented by the spiral.

Scientific research, especially in high energy physics, seems to support the idea that there is an urge within nature to achieve regularity in the face of primal chaos. Synchronistic events could be the clues that point to the existence of underlying, congruous connecting principles in the universe, providing evidence, as the Jungian analyst and internationally known lecturer Jean Shinoda Bolen said, for an 'underlying matrix or Tao'. In her book, 'The Tao of Psychology: synchronicity and the self' (1980), Bolen, clinical professor of psychiatry at the University of California Medical Centre, stated: 'Synchronistic events offer us perceptions that may be useful in our psychological and spiritual growth and may reveal to us, through intuitive knowledge, that our lives have meaning.'

For synchronicity to happen, the spaces between individuals and things, rather than being empty, must somehow afford a connecting link or themselves be a transmitting medium. Jung, of course, posited the collective unconscious, and synchronicity was his word for Tao. It reminds us of the idea of an 'information' medium between or 'behind' elementary particles, and of a 'superspectrum' of radiations which produce paranormal phenomena. Could this medium simply be consciousness itself?

At the quantum level, the world of the sub-atomic particles, there is no longer any distinction between energy and matter, and our bodies and everything around them are mainly made up of the spaces between these particles (rather than the particles themselves) in which electromagnetic fields are interacting and vibrating at extremely high frequencies. To put it another way, it seems we are composed mostly of 'nothing' at all! It is not surprising, then, that some sub-molecular physicists are now more interested in this 'nothing' – the space between the particles – than the particles themselves.

As don Juan tells Carlos in 'Tales of Power', we are simply perceivers, an awareness. 'We are not objects, we have no solidity,' says don Juan. 'The world of objects and solidity is a way of making our passage on earth convenient.' And at the sub-quantum level, the suggested realm of consciousness, there is no longer any way of distinguishing between space and time, or cause and effect.

Professor Bohm pointed out that at this level, cause and effect are illusion, just as at the quantum level the illusion of the solidity of our bodies and the world around us is revealed. It leads us to the view that consciousness, taken as the capability of a system to respond to stimuli, is the extreme substratum of matter, and that through our consciousness we create the illusion of space and time, cause and effect. Jung hinted at this when he said that synchronistic phenomena cannot in principle be associated with any concepts of causality, that in fact they lay beyond space and time, and cause and effect.

Jung also contended that the old theory of correspondence was based on the experience of synchronistic connections, and that synchronicity was a modern differentiation of what he described as the 'obsolete concept of correspondence, sympathy and harmony'. One would argue, perhaps, only with the adjective 'obsolete', for the Hermetic philosophy may yet be regaining its relevance.

Synchronicity was to space, time and causality what the one-dimensionality of time was to the three-dimensionality of space, Jung felt. He added that if the latest conclusions of science were coming nearer and

144

nearer to a unitary idea of being, which they now undoubtedly are, characterised by space and time on the one hand and causality and synchronicity on the other, then that had nothing to do with materialism. Rather, it seemed to show that there was a chance of getting rid of the incommensurability between the observed and the observer.

Arthur Koestler, in 'The Roots of Coincidence', an attempt to give extrasensory perception a basis in quantum physics, suggested that symbols such as the spiral provided patterns of behaviour for all human beings in archetypal situations. In such situations, the unconscious archetypes invaded consciousness, carrying strong emotions and, owing perhaps to the archetype's indifference to physical space and time, facilitated the occurrence of synchronistic events. The dustjacket of the 1972 Hutchinson edition of 'The Roots of Coincidence' features two spirals, one a mirror image of the other.

Koestler's next book, 'The Challenge of Change' (1973), related his study of coincidences to the synchronicity theories of Jung, Kammerer and Pauli. It was Kammerer who first recorded and analysed meaningful coincidences, suggesting that these events indicated an unrecognized law of nature which tended to make like and like cluster together. The name he gave to this phenomenon was 'seriality', and he defined it as 'a lawful recurrence, or clustering, in time and space whereby individual members of the sequence – as far as can be ascertained by careful analysis – are not connected by the same active source'.

In his 'Law of Seriality' (1919), Kammerer described seriality as 'the umbilical cord that connects thought, feeling, science and art with the womb of the universe which gave birth to them'.

Where Kammerer's seriality was more concerned with patterns and groupings of objects in the environment, Jung's synchronicity dealt with the relationship between subjectivity and the external world. But they were really both talking about the same thing. Jung enlarged on Kammerer's idea by suggesting that the mind was able to transcend normal concepts of space and time. It was the archetypes which were somehow responsible for gathering or connecting events unrelated by physical cause and effect energies, but were nevertheless connected by meaning for the observer. These events included precognition, and coincidences of dreams with incidents that later actually took place.

Koestler agreed that meaningful coincidences seemed to rest on archetypal situations. Certainly, as I researched this book, the coincidences kept piling up as I found more and more material representative of the ubiquitous spiral. To give just three examples: Caspersson's quartz-lensed microscope used for research into DNA and RNA, the Celtic double spirals I drew as a child without

145

knowing of their provenance, and the etymology which reveals that the word 'spiral' arises from linguistic origins rooted in ideas of creation and life-giving, inspiration and aspiration.

'The mystic's "oceanic feeling" is certainly on a higher turn of the spiral than the newborn infant's; the infant has not yet attained personal identity, the mystic and the medium have transcended it,' said Koestler. 'There are many turns of the spiral, from the slime-mould upwards, but at each turn we are confronted with the same polarity, the same Janus-faced holons, one face of which says I am the centre of the world, the other, I am a part in search of the whole.'

In nature, as we have seen, a small number of basic shapes and patterns occur in widely different contexts. As there is a complex network of acausal pattern correspondences throughout the structure of the universe it does not seem too far-fetched to think that events might occur in a similar way, both on an everyday and on a historical scale. Ancient astronomers were not so naïve as to think that time moved around and around in circles with the same situations duplicating themselves. The movement was thought of more as a developing spiral, thus intuitively heralding (for one thing) the discovery of the actual motion of our planet around the Sun made by modern astronomers, but more importantly promising the rediscovery of the relevance of this universal pattern.

Jung came up with the phrase 'magic causality' to describe the possibility of event patterning: a small deviation in the pattern of events holding sway at a particular moment could affect the overall situation and make a new pattern, and this new pattern might have the power to attract into relation with itself other events distant in space and time. It seemed to Jung that synchronicity represented a 'direct act of creation' manifesting itself as chance. It told us something about the nature of the unconscious archetype, and perhaps vice versa. Jung investigated the I Ching, the ancient Chinese method of divination within which yin and yang, the negative and positive forces of life, are paramount in importance, and the idea of synchronicity taken for granted, the method designed to interpret the meanings of coincidence. The psychical researcher and author Renee Haynes, who wrote a history of the Society for Psychical Research, commented: 'It is quality, meaning, that flashes like a shooting star through synchronicity.'

Wolfgang Pauli, who when still a student published a masterly exposition of the theory of relativity, went on to be the first to recognise the existence of the neutrino, an uncharged and massless sub-atomic particle. He first discussed the concept of synchronicity with Jung in the 1930s when he consulted the psychologist about his drink and marital problems. Pauli knew Jung had discovered something crucial in his concept of synchronicity, because he had begun to find deep meanings in his dreams. Dream symbols would synchronistically appear in letters Pauli received from colleagues and things that other researchers and friends said, and Pauli was gratified to find that important scientific insights could be achieved by allowing his mind to follow such non-rational and intuitive paths. It led him to explore the relationship between psyche and matter and his idea of 'resurrection of spirit within the world of matter'. Pauli, who evidently believed in psychology as much as he did in physics, sent Jung more than 1,000 dreams over the years and Jung published work which was based on some of them.

It amused Pauli that experimental equipment often broke down when he was around – a phenomenon which jocularly became known as the 'Pauli effect'. When, in 1948, at the foundation of the C G Jung institute, Pauli entered the room, one such effect occurred. A Chinese vase suddenly fell to the floor and water poured out, resulting in a flood. As Pauli at the time had begun to study the hermetic philosopher, Kabbalist and alchemist Robert Fludd (1574–1637), who wrote his name in Latin as Robertus de Fluctibus, this was a classic synchronistic event, with significance for the future scientific challenges which would be facing the institute.

> 'It is my personal opinion that in the science of the future reality will neither be "psychic" nor "physical" but somehow both and somehow neither.'
>
> Wolfgang Pauli

Jung's message was that as nowadays man is threatening himself with destruction, so we are experiencing a fundamental reassertion of our instincts in various forms, the psychological manifestations of which are the archetypes – no useless relics but living entities which can cause the pre-formation of numinous ideas ahead of our actual intellectual level. Jung felt that this was just what our times needed. It follows, then, that understanding the cosmic symbolism of spirality can be a means of raising the level of our consciousness, helping us to see the divinity within ourselves, and leading us towards a more enlightened way of life. Without the recognition of spirality, none of the ideas presented in this book would have been placed into a relationship, or their associative characteristics perceived. It did not appear beyond the range of possibility, said Jung, that we stood on the threshold of a new spiritual epoch, and that from the depths of our psychic life new spiritual forms would be born.

Now it has become more and more apparent that we as human beings are affected in many ways by happenings in the universe at large. We take for granted the heat and light radiated by the Sun, and the Moon's gravitational effect on the tides in the seas and oceans of the world. Sunspots are perhaps the most obvious of the adverse extra-terrestrial influences on our lives, their cycles interfering with our weather and communications.

We are also beginning to realise the possible implications of build-ups in gravitational forces exerted by the positioning of other planets in the solar system relative to the Earth and the Sun, and the effects of the waxing and waning of the Moon on human minds – after all, our bodies are 80 per cent water and so could be subject to 'tides' just as the oceans are.

Further, the oscillating electromagnetic fields of which we are ultimately constructed are doubtless affected by such outside fields, generated magnetically or gravitationally, in space. In the longer term, there are the effects of cosmic radiation which could emanate, say, from the supernova explosion of a neighbouring star, or of interstellar dust clouds as the Sun carries its family of planets in orbit through the spiral arm of the galaxy, perhaps having created ice ages on Earth in the past each time these clouds blocked the Sun's warmth.

The Earth, therefore, and mankind, are in no way separate from the universe, but inextricably bound up with it, as quantum science has also shown, and even the distant stars, probably collectively rather than individually, must be capable of some influence on us, however subtle.

This general notion has been supported by important investigations carried out by the South African-born astronomer and astrophysicist Dr Percy Seymour, a former principal lecturer in astronomy at the University of Plymouth, England, where he has carried out research into magnetic fields, and a researcher at the Royal Observatory, Greenwich. As a respected scientist he has bravely broken with scientific orthodoxy to claim that astrology could have some basis in fact.

In his book, 'The Scientific Proof of Astrology' (2004), he puts forward the theory that the human nervous system can act as an antenna through which some of the vibrations in the Earth's magnetic field can be detected. The geomagnetic field has fluctuations which are linked to the Sun and the Moon, and to the turning of the Earth on its own axis. In addition to this, there are further subtle variations linked to the sunspot cycle. Dr Seymour proposes that, in turn, this cycle is linked to the movements of the planets, including the Earth, around the Sun.

'This means that the whole solar system is playing a "symphony" on the magnetic field of the earth,' he says. 'According to the theory I have proposed, we are all genetically "tuned" to receive a different set of "melodies" from this symphony... It is in the womb that some of the "magnetic music of the spheres" becomes etched on our brains. The first role of our particular response to this music is to provide the cue for our entry onto the stage of the world. At later stages in life, when the solar system "plays our tune" again on the magnetic field of the Earth, it evokes these memories and our response may influence the way we act in a given situation.'

Seymour's challenging view is that 'serious' astrology, as opposed to the simplistic Sun-sign horoscopes found in newspapers and magazines, is an attempt to understand our own internal schedules formed over long periods of time and which we inherit genetically. He thinks that the fluctuations in the geomagnetic field synchronise the internal biological clocks of the foetus which control the moment of birth. The 'tuning of the foetal magnetic antenna' is carried out by the inherited genes, and this to some extent will influence personality characteristics. The positions of the planets at birth do not alter what we have inherited genetically, but instead 'label' our basic inherited characteristics of personality.

Cautious support for Seymour's ideas has come from an unexpected quarter – no less than Richard Dawkins in his role as Professor for the Public Understanding of Science. Dawkins once said that astrologers ought to be prosecuted under the Trades Descriptions Act, but has now gone on record as saying that Seymour's approach sounds interesting. Astrologers, naturally, are delighted by Seymour's claims.

Recall that, as Jung said, there are as many archetypes as there are typical situations in life. Continual repetition has imprinted these experiences into our psychic make-up, not at first in the form of meaningful images, but as forms promising the possibility of a certain mode of perception and expression. When a situation, psychological or otherwise, occurs which corresponds to a given archetype – say that represented by an astrological sign – then that archetype is activated and a compulsiveness appears with the momentum of an instinctual drive.

The effect on human lives of the precession of the equinoxes is spread over the length of the Great Year, the 26,000-year duration of which, like the normal year, is divided into twelve Platonic 'months', each one lasting about 2,160 years, and into 360 'days', each one lasting 72 years, roughly the Biblical 'three score years and ten' of the average human life span.

The Sun appears to be in a different sign of the zodiac in each month of the Great Year, remaining in each house for the requisite two millennia: every zodiacal sign being an archetypal image in its own right.

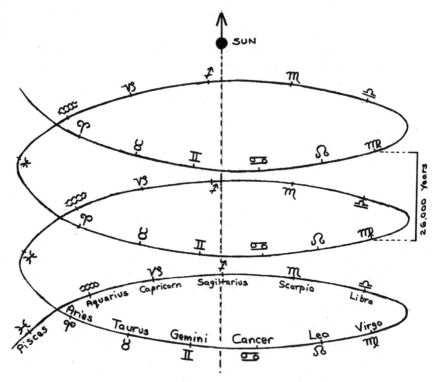

The spiral progression of the Great, or Platonic, years with each zodiacal sign recurring on a higher turn every 26,000 years.

Just as personal characteristics and attitudes seem to be determined by one's birth sign, so are the general characteristics of the various ages through history indicated by the house which the Sun occupies for the respective 2,160-year periods. For example, the Age of Leo (10800–8600BC) saw the rise of Sun worship and the divinity of kingship, its peoples building great temples, such as those at Tiahuanaco in the Andes, orientated to the rising and setting of the Sun at the winter and summer solstices. The Age of Cancer (8600–6500BC) saw the spread of the cult of the Great Mother goddess, identified with the Moon, in Asia, the Mediterranean area, and in western Europe and Britain.

In the Age of Gemini (6500–4300BC) there is evidence of dual orga-nisation in ancient civilizations, such as the Phoenicians, who worshipped dual deities, and of the invention of writing. The Age of Taurus (4300–2100BC) brought the cult of the bull to civilisation, and societies strove to give their ideas permanent expression through such structures as the Pyramids and the great stone monuments of Britain, as well as burgeoning artistic activities. In the Age of Aries (2100BC–50AD) a more monotheistic concept of God emerged, replacing the bull with the ram as sacred animal and sacrificial offering, and the period was marked by aggressive expansion and conquest as exemplified by the Greek and Roman empires.

As with personal natures, the ages are influenced not only by the sign through which the Sun is passing, but also by that of its polar opposite and the ruling planet of each pair of signs. Once the 26,000-year cycle has been completed, it begins again, although I believe it is best understood, again, in terms of a spiral progression through time with each age having its counterpart in a past and future Great Year, where the prevalent characteristics are displayed but modified with each succession.

More importantly for today, each time the Sun moves from one sign to another – and at present it is moving from the sign of Pisces, the Fishes, to Aquarius, the Man – there is an upheaval in human consciousness spread over hundreds of years as the retreating zodiacal influences of one age are met by the advancing influences of the next.

Astrologically, Jung saw it as a manifestation of 'psychic changes' which always occur at the end of each 'month' in the Great Year. In our present epoch, at the turn of the millennium, we are seeing the end of a Platonic month and a uniquely awesome stage in human history which has preoccupied the minds of seers and prophets for thousands of years as being the time of the 'end of the world' or 'doomsday', to be brought about by natural or man-made catastrophe. Compounding our problem is the certitude that, as Jung knew, so many people today are living without their souls, and are generally bereft of any sense of other worlds.

> 'Either brace yourself for elimination, or else your hearts must have the courage for the changing of the guards... Peace will come with tranquillity and splendour on the wheels of fire...'
>
> Bob Dylan, *The Changing of the Guards,* 1978

Lyall Watson referred to 'a sort of changing of the guards by the gods which takes place wherever there is a long-lasting transformation of the collective psyche'. With the death of one age, we witness another rising Phoenix-like, either literally or at least metaphorically, from the ashes of the first. In the Age of Pisces, where we have seen the rise of Christianity (Christ, the 'fisher of men', symbolised by a fish) we have also experienced the suffering and self-undoing which are special characteristics of this sign.

Pisces has qualities which can transport the soul to pinnacles of mystical experience or send it plummeting to the caverns of despair, extremes only too recognisable in man's behaviour during the past 2,000 years, and which have led some to wonder whether man is basically a flawed or somehow incomplete being.

Alternatively, perhaps it is as the English philosopher, novelist and critic Colin Wilson (1931–) has suggested, that, gradually, over thousands of years, our intuitive right-brain lost out to the rational left-brain, so that in modern man such attributes as precognition, telepathy, astral projection, telekinesis and so on – indeed, all the manifestations of the paranormal – are the remnants of the once-dominant faculties of our ancestors.

Possibly, some 12,000 years ago, a couple of thousand years after the end of the last ice age, there was a civilisation – Atlantis we may like to call it – where the intuitive right-brain-dominated way of thinking was the norm. After the destruction of this civilisation, survivors passed on knowledge to successive societies, notably those in Ancient Egypt and Central America. The conclusion seems inescapable that the consciousness of our distant ancestors was of a quintessentially different quality to ours today.

I mention Colin Wilson at this point because it was my first meeting with him in 1999 that inspired me to persevere with the completion of this book, the idea for which I had already had for a number years and on which I had carried out a modicum of research. The development of the 'Outsider' theme in Wilson's many books over almost half a century seems to me capable of being represented as a series of ascending turns on a literary and philosophical spiral affording new vantage points from which his work has been refined and deepened.

As Itzhak Bentov realised, knowledge moves 'in an ever-expanding upward spiral, which allows us to see from the higher turn of the spiral our previous knowledge in a broader perspective'. As Newton's mechanics became a 'special case' within Einstein's theory of relativity, for example, so Einstein's theory is becoming a 'special case' in a new science taking account of both mental and physical phenomena.

For the past 200 years, as the incoming Aquarian Age has begun to make its presence felt, we have found ourselves subjected to a dizzying acceleration in the pace of life and an accompanying revolution in scientific and spiritual thought which has not only affected people's ways of life everywhere but has also, through Darwin, Einstein, Jung and others, begun to unravel the mysteries of humankind and the cosmos. It could be that, as Wilson believes, the events of the past two centuries place us on the brink of an evolutionary leap forward. And an element within such a leap would be the grasping once again of the nature of the forgotten knowledge of those ancient civilisations which embraced the secret of cosmic harmony and its exact vibrations, and enabled its peoples to feel a part of nature instead of experiencing alienation from it.

At present, we discover ourselves in transit between two 'stations' – in the Scorpio decanate, to give the position its astrological term – leaving behind the confused emotions of the Piscean Age and travelling towards the traditional age of wisdom and enlightenment, that of Aquarius, the sign of humanity and brotherhood, of vision and unity, whose symbol is also the phoenix.

In between the two we are undergoing all manner of crises and revolutions which, threatening the very foundations of our civilisation, are the trademarks of the passing of one age and the birth, or rebirth, of the next. What the ultimate cost of arriving at the new age is likely to be in terms of human anguish and planetary disruption remains to be seen, for there are indications that we may be heading for a final crisis of unprecedented proportion in the near future, which perhaps has to take place in order to 'wipe the slate clean' before a more beneficial order can be born. We find ourselves in an existential crux.

Yet why would the universe want to risk destruction of the very consciousness of itself which it has taken billions of years to create? As Plato said: 'Things are far better taken care of than we can possibly imagine.'

The theme of this book stands wholly against the pessimistic view of our place in the universe which has become so prevalent in our time – the 'fallacy of insignificance', to use one of Wilson's key terms – that we are merely on a 'dust-mote' planet in orbit around an average star in a run-of-the-mill galaxy; that there are countless other planets, stars and galaxies out there; that although Earth has life, it may not be that unusual or important, and that because the distances are so vast there is such little chance of locating intelligent life elsewhere that we might as well be alone in the cosmos; in short, that the universe is out to persuade us that we are nothing very special.

Readers will not be surprised to learn that I have always rejected such a defeatist attitude. Certainly, the astronomy of Copernicus (1473–1543), with its heliocentric system, overturned that of Ptolemy (c100–170), which for a thousand years had placed the Earth at the

153

centre of the universe. Inevitably, the Copernican revolution dislodged human beings from the centre of the physical universe, but at the same time it reconvened our relationship to the universe on a different level. The new astronomy after Copernicus not only realigned the human subject as a rational being capable of understanding the structure of the cosmos through mathematical endeavour, it also paved the way for the realisation that, as referred to in the previous chapter, we are the universe contemplating itself – indeed, a privileged position.

However, I do believe we need a more spiritual response to the dangers inherent in the technological society and the shallowness of modernity; a more organic way of living needs to be found if we are to attain that crucial point of *eucatastrophe*, the turning back from the brink of disaster. Yet I am of the view that the unconscious forces released by millennial dread – including the whole of the 'New Age' phenomenon – must be shaped by and applied with a certain practicality if they are to be of any lasting use to us; we must try to formulate what I would term a transcendental pragmatism in order to aid the evolution of consciousness, and the works of Jung and Wilson, in particular, provide us with the impetus to move in this direction.

Indeed, I would hope that this book may be seen as something of an example of the approach which I envisage, entering into a region of experience in which the rational and the non-rational are unafraid to cohabit and can produce new sets of correspondences and connections leading to a deeper insight into the way of our universe – transcendental in the sense of a philosophy that lays emphasis on intuition as a means of knowing a spiritual reality, and which embraces the belief that divinity pervades nature and humanity; and pragmatic in the idea that a theory or concept should be evaluated in terms of how it works, what its consequences are, and what are its standards for action and thought.

Wilson's 'new existentialism', a philosophy of intuition which counters the pessimistic and fatalistic Continental 'school' of existentialism of the mid-20th century, is already setting down the foundations for fresh paths of philosophical and psychological inquiry in the 21st century, and offers a paradigm for a renewed humanity. Underlying all his works is an optimism and a faith in the power and potential of the human mind to rise above the mediocre or the malevolent to new and higher levels of awareness, and to press against and challenge the boundaries of everyday consciousness. Hopefully, we can exploit this potential to regain faith in our 'ancient' future.

Central in Wilson's work is the question of how people can achieve those strange moments of inner freedom, of sheer delight, of 'peak experience', or 'ecstasy', when we feel our energies are more than adequate to cope with any challenge, those moments of 'pure joy in which we experience an almost god-like sensation of power or freedom'. Such occasions are in stark contrast to normal consciousness in which we seem to sense our energies are never quite up to the mark, or feel ourselves to be in the grip of impersonal forces much stronger than ourselves. To give some literary examples, these occasions are akin to William Wordsworth's 'spots of time', Thomas Hardy's 'moments of vision' and James Joyce's 'epiphanies', and Wilson's view is that our personal development depends on what might be termed such 'intensity experiences'. For me, contemplation of the elegance and beauty of the spiral form and its breathtaking plenitude in nature, as well as its existential symbolism, is more than capable of inducing that sensation.

Certainly, I would imagine Wilson to be among those who understand that the experience of the supernatural conjoins with the extremes of human passion. For he has also written extensively about the paranormal, the effects of which he is sure are linked to the mind's untapped potential, and one finds the essence of his work in the fusion of its two major strands, existentialism and occultism. He is one of the few thinkers who has stood out against the endemic pessimism and defeatism of our times, and their tendency to reject substance and meaning in favour of image and ephemera. Meaning is the antidote to pessimism and to the sense of the absurdity and pointlessness of existence.

Jung, too, inferred the existence of a transcendental meaning independent of consciousness, largely by observation of those phenomena he called 'synchronistic'. This is why another term for synchronicity is 'meaningful coincidence'.

The general superficiality and nihilism of our times, our Faustian obsession with materialism, amounts to a kind of rejection, or at least a willing, or even wilful, diminution of consciousness, which is, of course, a disastrous backward step, a spurning of the spiral's promise. As Einstein said: 'The man who regards his own life and that of his fellow creatures as meaningless is not only unfortunate but almost disqualified for life.'

These times we live in must be the most frightening but surely the most exciting and stimulating ever to have confronted mankind, standing as we do, however shakily, on the brink of a new consciousness. I hope that the seven chapters of this book have succeeded in presenting complementary and integrated aspects of the personal vision I have of the deep significance and meaningfulness of the spiral's omnipresence in human and cosmic terms as the pattern of existence.

Moving ever upward on the spiral course of destiny, hopefully with the promise of spiritual renaissance, it can only be through future generations on this 're-volutionary' path that we will start to understand and begin to realise the complete potential of the privileged place and powers which the universe has bestowed upon us.

'...the quest for ultimate Unity shared by the physicist, the mystic and the parapsychologist; a kind of unity which can only be attained by a detour through diversity, on a higher turn of the spiral.'

Arthur Koestler, *The Roots of Coincidence*, 1972

Appendix 1

Spirals and altered states of consciousness

Many anthropologists and other researchers today believe that, more than 30,000 years ago, human beings came to value hallucinatory experiences and regularly used plants with psychotropic properties to trigger them – indeed, that the origin of shamanism, and of religious and artistic sensibility, lies in the neurological ability to enter altered states of consciousness (ASCs).

Such states could also be induced by rhythmic drumming and/or dancing, self-mutilation, fasting, hyperventilation and various other techniques not requiring the use of naturally occurring hallucinogenic substances such as peyote, datura root, ayahuasca, ibogaine and the psilocybin 'magic' mushroom.

In his book, 'Supernatural: meetings with the ancient teachers of mankind' (Century, 2005), Graham Hancock (www.grahamhancock. com) champions the work of Professor David Lewis-Williams, the South African anthropologist who, in the 1980s, became the prime exponent of the theory that ASCs in ancient man, including deep trances, explain the odd ideas about supernatural realms and other-wordly beings which are at the foundation of all religions. Indeed, the word 'trance' comes from the Latin *transire* meaning to 'go across', as in the word 'entrance', which links with the ideas of the Spiral or World Mountain, sacred spots where above and below, Earth and Heaven, meet.

Professor Lewis-Williams, of the Rock Art Research Institute at Witwatersrand University, realised that modern neuropsychological investigations of entoptic phenomena, which he argued were attributable to the structure of the nervous system, could explain the strange symbols and creatures – many of them part human and part animal – depicted in

157

prehistoric cave art which appeared from 35,000 years ago in Europe and from 27,000 years ago in Africa.

Entoptic is the term used to denote visual images occurring or originating inside the eye, and which can arise from the optic system at any point between the eyeball and the cerebral cortex, and sometimes also referred to as flicker phosphenes. If you close your eyes, and rub your eyeball gently, you should see simple patterns of light which occur because you are stimulating a part of your retina, even though you are not actually looking at anything. Similar phosphenes are observed by people who have taken marijuana or psychedelic drugs, such as LSD, or when they have been exposed to flickering light – and one of the most commonly recurring patterns is that of a spiral.

The first serious study of entoptic phenomena was made in the 1920s by Heinrich Kluver (1897–1979), the German neurologist and experimental psychologist who became a professor of biological sciences at the University of Chicago.

His work involved the connection between entoptic imagery and ASCs induced by hallucinogenic drugs, in this case mescaline, a psychotropic alkaloid produced from the buttons of the peyote cactus. Kluver took mescaline himself as part of his experiments, as well as interviewing dozens of people about their experiences under the effects of the drug.

He found that in the early stages of the mescaline 'trip', people reported seeing abstract geometrical images which fell into four main types, or what he called 'form constants': spirals, tunnels, cobwebs and honeycombs. Similar hallucinations had been reported by people on the brink of falling asleep or waking, after being given an anaesthetic, and when meditating or undergoing a 'near-death experience' (NDE). Kluver's findings, which established categories of repeated images, were confirmed and expanded upon by other psychiatrists and neuropsychologists in subsequent decades.

Anthropologist Gerardo Reichel-Dolmatoff's study of 1975 revealed that phosphenic patterns, including the spiral, dominated contemporary rock paintings of the Tukano indians of Colombia, South America. As Graham Hancock records, this study brought into evidence the laboratory experiments of Max Knoll who used electrical stimulation of the brain to induce phosphenes in more than a thousand Western volunteers who then drew what they had seen. The similarities between the two sets of patterns was striking, not just in the spirals, but also in sets of wavy lines and diamond, triangular and star shapes.

Clearly, entoptic imagery also has implications for later prehistoric art of the kind that decorates neolithic monuments such as those at

Newgrange in Ireland, and Carnac in Brittany, and some scholars have speculated that hallucinogenic mushrooms may have had a role in the conception of this art. Graham, who kindly allowed me to quote from 'Supernatural: meetings with the ancient teachers of mankind', comments that it is as though 'the great project of the painted caves never quite died out but somehow re-emerged among the megaliths thousands of years later'.

Graham reports that, in research in a number of countries, people experiencing ASCs go through a series of stages with entoptic patterns at the beginning of the sequence and powerful 'iconic' visions of animals, humans, hybrid beings and so on, at the end. 'Regardless of cultural differences among the subjects, the shift into this last stage was often said to have been accompanied by powerful fast-moving imagery of a spiral or vortex, sometimes in the form of tunnels, funnels, alleys and cones,' he says. 'The very universality of these spiral/vortex images suggests an origin within the structure of the optic system . . .'

It could be that the uses of hallucinogens, or even unaided artistic inspiration, trigger ancient archetypal symbols in the collective unconscious which are usually excluded from everyday consciousness. One recalls, for example, that the religion of the Dogon people of West Africa is characterised by the worship of ancestors and spirits, and their rituals involve impersonation of their ancestors with the use of masks which are well-known for their spiral motifs linked to genesis myths (the Dogon believe the Sirius binary star system to be the axis of the universe, and that all matter and souls are generated from it in a vast spiral movement).

However, Graham suggests that rather than the brain simply being a 'factory' that manufactures hallucinations, there is a possibility that it acts as a receiver which, during ASCs, is retuned to pick up frequencies, dimensions and entities which are 'completely real in their own way but that are normally inaccessible to us'.

He also speculates, referring to a number of other researchers in the field, that DNA is driven by intelligence and that it contains a message from our 'ancient teachers' which our consciousness can access through ASCs – especially when the function of 97 per cent of our DNA is unknown (only three per cent comprises genes). If he is right, then the implications of this for the further significance of the spiral form to human existence could not be more profound. Remember that Francis Crick, the Nobel Prize-winning biologist, co-discoverer of the DNA structure, was under the influence of LSD in 1953 at the very moment he visualised the double helix design.

Graham, who travelled to Peru to join indigenous shamans in the ceremonial drinking of the ayahuasca brew in order to find out for himself what the effects were, experienced a vision of snakes winding around each other 'like the DNA double helix' (or the caduceus of Hermes). The American anthropologist Michael Harmer, who in 1961 was one of the first Westerners to experiment with ayahuasca in the Amazon, saw dragon-like creatures which, he learned, had come to Earth from space and were inside all forms of life, including man. Another anthropologist taking ayahuasca found himself in the presence of two enormous snakes which talked to him.

It is easy to see how such accounts resonate back through the pages of 'Spiral Way' where I have commented upon the relevance of spirality to the snake, serpent and dragon. Serpents and snakes are a prominent feature of ayahuasca visions; not for nothing is it known as the 'serpent drug'.

Rick Strassman, professor of psychiatry at the University of New Mexico School of Medicine, published the findings of a government-backed hallucinogen research programme in his 2001 book, 'DMT: the spirit molecule' (Park Street Press, Rochester, Vermont). Volunteers subjected themselves to doses of DMT (dimethyltryptamine), the psychoactive ingredient of ayahuasca, thereby boosting the minute levels which already exist in the brain, blood and spinal fluid. Several of the volunteers found themselves having intense visions of 'spirals of DNA' and 'threads of DNA'. Strassman says that the evolutionary or adaptive justification for DMT might be to retune the brain to different levels of reality, the realms associated with shamanic and spiritual and religious disciplines.

An alternative explanation as to why hallucinations occur, and how they may be a natural consequence of the architecture of our brains (as Professor Lewis-Williams thought), has been given by the mathematician and neuroscientist Jack Cowan, of the University of Chicago, who in 2001 reported on an artificial brain he had constructed which was able to re-create hallucinations similar to those experienced by users of psychotropic drugs. In 1977, he had realised that some of Kluver's illustrations resembled convection patterns, and this led him to formulate a new theory based on more than 20 years of research.

Convection patterns in hot water involve a complex interplay of opposing forces, causing spontaneous patterns to emerge, such as rolling tubes of water forming parallel stripes, or square or hexagonal cells. Similarly, Cowan believed that hallucinations might be spontaneous patterns of activity in the brain caused by the interplay between neurons which are either becoming excited or are calming down.

One action, like the buoyancy of water, tended to excite the neurons while the other, like the diffusion of heat, had a calming effect. Cowan thought this could happen in the primary visual cortex, a layer of tissue two to three millimetres thick at the back of the brain serving as the first layer of processing for images gathered by the retina. This is within the neocortex, the area of the brain which, as we have seen in Chapter Six: Coil of Life, evolved most recently (about half a million years ago), and led to the development of human intelligence.

To test his ideas, Cowan designed a mathematical model of the primary visual cortex, and then gave it a dose of 'virtual LSD' and, as in a real brain, the model showed that each neuron tended to excite its neighbours and inhibit those a little further away. Normally, a visual neuron will not fire unless the input from the retina and from its neighbours exceeds a critical threshold. But the hallucinogen allows neurons to fire when there is nothing in the visual field; it lowers the threshold so that excitation exceeds inhibition and waves of activity begin to form, as when the heat under a saucepan of water is increased. LSD, for example, does this by making the brain stem secrete less of the inhibitory chemical serotonin.

The first patterns to appear are similar to those of the heated water – parallel stripes, chequerboards and hexagons. Cowan's computer model demonstrated that hallucinated parallel lines appeared to be drawn into the centre, thereby creating the impression of a spiral or tunnel, or indeed a spiral tunnel, and checks and hexagons spiralled in the same way. This was due to the fact that the patterns were in the cortex and not in the retina, and the tendency of the cortex is to emphasise objects close to the centre of the field of vision, where our sight is sharp, while relatively little is made available for peripheral vision.

Cowan's model reproduced most of the hallucinatory patterns documented by Kluver and others. It seemed, therefore, that three-quarters of a century later, two of Kluver's form constants had been explained: users of hallucinogens see spirals and tunnels (or spiral tunnels) – and those undergoing NDEs commonly encounter the 'tunnel of light' illusion – because these are the objects in the outside world which fit the patterns of the firing of neurons in the cortex. The significance of the spiral form imposing itself here, with its attendant numinous consequences for those observing these patterns, hardly needs to be underlined.

Although Cowan believes such hallucinations are the result of brain cells becoming unstable and producing certain patterns, he thinks they could offer a route into those profound depths of the mind which harbour emotions and conscious thought, for cognition and emotion, as well as self-awareness, are also affected by the hallucinatory experience. Hallucinations could be the place to start looking for an answer to the question of how far the mind, with its rich inner world of experiences which give us our sense of identity and of self, is a product of physiological processes in the brain. As the neocortex is the newest part of the brain, in evolutionary terms, its cellular structure is fairly uniform, even if its various functions are quite different, which means that it might be possible to extend known values about, say, activities in the primary visual cortex, to adjacent areas.

All this is not to suggest, of course, that entoptic phenomena and/or hallucinations, whether or not induced by psychoactive agents, have been the sole or even the primary source of spiral imagery in human culture. ASCs, whether entered by botanical, geodetic or physiological means, are obviously not essential to the manifestation of the spiral pattern, or the perception of its significance. The spiral is an intrinsic part of nature, as we are. However, ASCs do seem to present a substantial clue as to how and why the spiral became associated, as a numen, with ritual, religious and artistic practice down the ages.

Appendix 2

Precession and the Binary Companion Theory

Scientists have speculated about the existence of another body orbiting the Sun for a century at least, and there has been increased interest in the subject since the 1980s, with a variety of theories being put forward. In 2001, the Binary Research Institute was set up in California to support and fund research on the hypothesis that the Sun is part of a binary star system, in which it and a companion star orbit about a common centre of gravity, with the respective orbits overlapping.

In such a system, the stars can be of similar or differing sizes and orbits can be as short as a few days or as long as thousands of years. The short orbits are easy to detect, while the long ones can be extremely difficult, and some probably impossible to detect because of the extraordinarily long observation periods required.

However, the institute hopes to find evidence for the binary theory, and show that the motion of the Sun along a binary orbital path can account for the precessional motion of the Earth better than the conventional scientific explanation involving the Earth's 'wobble' and the gravitational effects of the Sun and Moon. If there is a binary companion, then the spiral movement of our solar system through space would become even more complex as it would be interacting with a similar movement followed by the companion star and any planets it might have in orbit.

The founder of the Binary Research Institute, Walter W. Cruttenden, a former investment banker and venture capitalist, believes that the rise and fall of the ages, as determined by the Platonic or Great Year, may be tied to solar system motion, and is sympathetic to the idea that ancient cultures were far more advanced than generally acknowledged, and that there is scientific evidence to support the notion of a great cycle with subtle energies that affect human consciousness. Cruttenden's book 'Lost Star of Myth and Time' was published by St Lynn's Press in October, 2005.

The institute's website (www.binaryresearchinstitute.org) claims that scientific evidence, as well as new mathematical models and an expanding knowledge of binary star systems, call into question the long-accepted 'lunisolar' theory and lends surprising support to the binary view.

Researchers have found that a binary orbit motion of the Sun and solar system is a simpler way to reproduce the same observable phenomena without any of the problems now known to be associated with current precession theory. They hope to locate the Sun's stellar companion with the use of a 'virtual observatory', a collection of interacting astronomical databases accessed by special software run on powerful computers. As a 'virtual telescope', this system is capable of processing many years of amassed astronomical information in order to find patterns or tracks which would point to a faint star likely to be the companion.

While there is no obvious visible companion, there could be a dark binary, such as a brown dwarf, or even a relatively small black hole, either of which might be very difficult to detect without accurate and lengthy analysis. Beyond direct detection, one way to determine if we are in a binary system is to find out if the Sun is curving through space.

See also science writer Andy Lloyd's Dark Star website at www.darkstar1.co.uk which includes scientific, mythological, esoteric and messianic indexes. Lloyd's book 'Dark Star: the Planet X evidence', which assesses the case for a binary system, was published by Timeless Voyager Press in October, 2005.

Lloyd says that brown dwarfs can provide enough heat and light for habitable environments on planets orbiting such failed stars, and predicts that the binary companion will be found in the Oort Cloud which makes up the bulk of the solar system's volume. The Oort Cloud is a postulated spherical cloud of comets located about one light year from the Sun, or about 1,000 times the distance to Pluto, the outermost planet, and is believed to be the source of all or most of the comets which enter the inner solar system.

Bibliography

1: INTO THE SWIRL

Ashe, Geoffrey. King Arthur's Avalon: the story of Glastonbury, Collins, 1957; The Ancient Wisdom, Macmillan, 1977; The Glastonbury Tor Maze, Gothic Image Publications, 1979.

Barrow, John D. The Artful Universe Expanded, Oxford University Press, 2005.

Blofeld, John. I Ching, the Book of Change, George Allen & Unwin, 1965.

Charpentier, Louis. The Mysteries of Chartres Cathedral, Rilko, 1972.

Clark, Graham. World Prehistory: in new perspective, Cambridge University Press, 1977.

Conway, David. Secret Wisdom: the occult universe explored, Jonathan Cape, 1985.

Gardiner, Philip and Osborn, Gary. The Serpent Grail: the truth behind the Holy Grail, the Philosopher's Stone and the Elixir of Life, Watkins Publishing, 2005.

Hayes, Michael. High Priests, Quantum Genes: science, religion and the theory of everything, Black Spring Press, 2004.

Holroyd, Stuart. Magic, Words and Numbers, Aldus Books, 1975.

Holroyd, Stuart and Powell, Neil. Mysteries of Magic, Aldus Books, 1975.

Jordan, Michael. Ceremonies for Life, Collins & Brown, 2001.

Mann, Nicholas R. The Isle of Avalon: sacred mysteries of Arthur and Glastonbury, Green Magic, 2001. Energy Secrets of Glastonbury Tor, Green Magic, 2004.

Michell, John. The View Over Atlantis, Sago Press, 1969; City of Revelation, Garnstone Press, 1972; A Little History of Astro-Archaeology, Thames & Hudson, 1977; New Light on the Ancient Mystery of Glastonbury, Gothic Image Publications, 1990.

Pennick, Nigel. The Ancient Science of Geomancy, Thames & Hudson, 1979.

Rawson, Philip and Legeza, Laszlo. Tao: the Chinese philosophy of time and change, Thames & Hudson, 1973.

Roberts, Anthony (ed). Glastonbury: ancient Avalon, new Jerusalem, Rider, 1977.

Roland, Paul. The Complete Kabbalah Course, Quantum, 2005.

Saunders, Kevin. Wiccan Spirituality: a magical attitude for the 21st century, Green Magic, 2002.

Saward, Jeff. Labyrinths & Mazes: the definitive guide to ancient & modern traditions, Gaia Books, 2003.

Skinner, Stephen. Terrestrial Astrology: divination by geomancy, Routledge & Kegan Paul, 1980.

Starhawk, The Spiral Dance: a rebirth of the ancient religion of the goddess, Harper San Francisco, 1979/1999.

Varley, Desmond. Seven: the number of creation, Bell & Sons, 1976.

Watts, Alan. The Two Hands of God: the myths of polarity, Collier USA, 1969; The Supreme Identity, Wildwood House, 1972; Tao: the watercourse way, Jonathan Cape, 1976.

Williams, Mary (ed). Glastonbury: a study in patterns, Rilko, 1969.

Wood, Michael. In Search of the First Civilisations, BBC Books, 1992/2005.

2: THE SPELL OF THE ARCHETYPE

Armstrong, Karen. The Spiral Staircase: a memoir, HarperCollins, 2004.

Clarke, J J. Jung and Eastern Thought, Routledge, 1994.

Erdinger, Edward F. Ego and Archetype, Shambhala, 1992 (orig. Putnam NY, 1972).

Hannah, Barbara. Jung: his life and work, Michael Joseph, 1977; Encounters with the Soul: active imagination as developed by C G Jung, Sigo Press, 1981.

Hitchcock, John. The Web of the Universe: Jung, the 'new physics' and human spirituality, Paulist Press, 1991.

Houston, Jean. The Hero and the Goddess: the Odyssey as mystery and initiation, Ballantine Books, 1992.

Jaffe, Aniela. The Myth of Meaning in the work of C G Jung. Translated by R F C Hull, Hodder & Stoughton, 1970.

Jung, Carl Gustav. The Collected Works, esp. Psychological Types (Vol 6), Synchronicity: an acausal connecting principle (Vol 8), The Archetypes and the Collective Unconscious (Vol 9), Psychology and Alchemy (Vol 12), The Symbolic Life: Miscellaneous Writings

(Vol 18), Routledge & Kegan Paul, 1977; Memories, Dreams, Reflections, Collins and Routledge & Kegan Paul, 1963; Man and his Symbols, Aldus Books, 1964; C G Jung Speaking: Interviews and Encounters, ed. William McGuire and R F C Hull, Thames and Hudson, 1978.

Schoch-Bodmer, Helen. Die Spirale als Symbol und als Strukturelment des Lebendigen, Schweizerische Zeitschriftfur Psychologie und ihre Anwendungen, Bern, 1945.

Jung, Emma and von Franz, Marie-Louise. The Grail Legend, Princeton University Press, 1998 (orig. 1960).

3: RITUAL, ART AND NATURE

Brown, Dan. The Da Vinci Code, Bantam Press, 2003.

Colegrave, Sukie. The Spirit of the Valley: androgyny and Chinese thought, Virago, 1979.

Colman, S and Coan, C A (ed). Nature's Harmonic Unity, Putnam USA, 1912.

Cook, T A. Spirals in Nature and Art, John Murray, 1903; The Curves of Life, Constable, 1914.

De Quincey, Thomas. Confessions of an English Opium Eater and Other Writings, ed. Aileen Ward, Signet Classics, 1966.

Hambridge, Jay. The Elements of Dynamic Symmetry, Dover, 1967, from The Diagonal, 1919, 1920.

Hancock, Graham. Fingerprints of the Gods: a quest for the beginning and the end, Heinemann, 1995; Supernatural: meetings with the ancient teachers of mankind, Century, 2005.

Knight, Christopher and Lomas, Robert. Uriel's Machine: the ancient origins of science, Arrow, 2004.

Lao Tzu. Tao Te Ching, Penguin, 1963.

Livio, Mario. The Golden Ratio: the story of Phi, the extraordinary number of nature, art and beauty, Review, 2002.

Marshall, Peter. Europe's Lost Civilisation: uncovering the mysteries of the megaliths, Headline, 2004.

Merton, Thomas. The Way of Chuan Tzu, Unwin Books, 1970.

Moore, Thomas. Dark Nights of the Soul, Piatkus, 2004.

Morgan, Sally. Spirals (World of Shapes series), Wayland, 1994.

Nicholl, Charles. Leonardo da Vinci: the flights of the mind, Allen Lane, 2004.

Purce, Jill. The Mystic Spiral: journey of the soul, Thames & Hudson, 1974.

Sagan, Carl. Cosmos, Macdonald, 1981.

Scarre, Chris (ed). The Human Past: world prehistory and the development of human societies, Thames & Hudson, 2005.

Stevens, Peter S. Patterns in Nature, Atlantic–Little Brown, 1974.

Thompson, D'Arcy Wentworth. On Growth and Form, abridged edition, Cambridge University Press, 1961 (orig. Cambridge, 1917).

Underwood, Guy. The Patterns of the Past, Pitman, 1969.

Weaver, Herbert. Divining the Primary Sense, Routledge & Kegan Paul, 1978.

Weintraub, Joseph. The Wit and Wisdom of Mae West, Cliffs Notes, 1981.

Williamson, Ray A. Living the Sky: the cosmos of the American indian, University of Oklahoma Press, 1987.

4: DRAGON MAGIC

Bailey, James. The Parish Church of St Mary & St David at Kilpeck, Five Seasons Press, Hereford, 2000.

Bord, Janet and Colin. Mysterious Britain, Paladin, 1974; The Secret Country, Paladin, 1978.

Broadhurst, Paul and Miller, Hamish. The Sun and the Serpent, Pendragon Press, 1989.

Brooks, Tom. The Hand of Man: Britain's prehistory decoded, Edward Gaskell, Devon, 2004.

Cope, Julian. The Megalithic European: the 21st century traveller in prehistoric Europe, Element, 2004; The Modern Antiquarian: a pre-millennial odyssey through megalithic Britain, Thorsons, 1998.

Dames, Michael. The Silbury Treasure: the Great Goddess rediscovered, Thames & Hudson, 1976 (reprint 2004).

Graves, Tom. Needles of Stone, Turnstone Press, 1978.

Heselton, Philip. Earth Mysteries, Element, 1991.

Hitching, Francis. Earth Magic, Cassell, 1976; The World Atlas of Mysteries, 1978.

Krupp, E C. In Search of Ancient Astronomies, Chatto & Windus, 1979.

Laidler, Keith. The Head of God: the lost treasure of the Templars, Phoenix, 2005.

Lethbridge, T C. Ghost and Divining Rod, 1963, ESP: Beyond Time and Distance, 1965, The Power of the Pendulum (with foreword by Colin Wilson) 1976, all Routledge & Kegan Paul.

Neumann, Erich. The Origins and History of Consciousness, H Karnac, 1989 (orig. 1949).

Newham, C A. The Astronomical Significance of Stonehenge, John Blackburn, 1972.

Paine, Crispin. Sacred Places: spirit and landscape, National Trust, 2004.

Pepper, Elizabeth and Wilcock, John. Magical and Mystical Sites: Europe and the British Isles, Weidenfeld & Nicolson, 1977.

Screeton, Paul. Quicksilver Heritage, Thorsons, 1974.

Spence, Lewis. The Mysteries of Britain, Rider, 1928.

Sullivan, Danny. Ley Lines: the greatest landscape mystery, Green Magic, 2004.

Watkins, Alfred. The Old Straight Track, Methuen, 1925.

The Dragon Isle:

Albin, J. History of the Isle of Wight, 1796.

Basford, H V. The Vectis Report: a survey of Isle of Wight archaeology, IW County Council, 1986.

Boase, Wendy. The Folklore of Hampshire and the Isle of Wight, Batsford, 1976.

Dennett, John. On the Barrows of the Isle of Wight, 1816.

Elder, Abraham. Tales and Legends of the Isle of Wight, 1839.

Frost, Richard. Isle of Wight Mysteries, Nigh & Sons, 1980.

Hargrove, Ethel C. Wanderings in the Isle of Wight, 1913.

Harris, Rendel. Egypt and the Isle of Wight, W Heffer & Sons, 1927.

Hawkes, Jacquetta. The Longstone, Antiquity no. 123, September 1957.

Hillier, George. The History and Antiquities of the Isle of Wight, 1855.

Hutchins, John. The History and Antiquities of the County of Dorset, vol 2, 1863, vol 3, 1868.

Kokeritz, Helge. The Placenames of the Isle of Wight, Uppsala, 1940.

Mantell, G. Mantell's Geology of the Isle of Wight, 1854.

Nelson & Sons. The Isle of Wight, its History, Topography and Antiquities, 1882.

Norman, Mark Wm. A Popular Guide to the Geology of the Isle of Wight, 1887.

Oglander, John. The Oglander Memoirs: extracts from the MSS of Sir John Oglander, 1888.

Peel, Edmund. The Fair Island, 1851.

Proceedings of the Prehistoric Society for 1960, New Series, vol XXVI, Excavation of a burial mound on Arreton Down, Isle of Wight.

Rhodes, H T F. The Satanic Mass, Rider, 1954.

Royal Commission on Historical Monuments, Long Barrows in Hampshire and the Isle of Wight.

Tomkins, Charles. A Tour to the Isle of Wight, 1796.

Victoria History of the Counties of England: Hampshire and the Isle of Wight, vol 5, Constable, 1912.

Walker, Robert. Phoenicia in Freshwater, 1892.

White, H J Osborne. A Short Account of the Geology of the Isle of Wight, HMSO, 1921.

Wilkins, Dr Ernest P. Geology, Antiquities and Topgraphy of the Isle of Wight, 1859.

Worsley's History of the Isle of Wight, 1781.

5: THE SPIRACULATE UNIVERSE

Bova, Ben. The New Astronomies, Dent, 1973.

Brockman, John (ed). Science at the Edge, Weidenfeld & Nicolson, 2004.

Calder, Nigel. The Key to the Universe: a report on the new physics, BBC, 1977; Einstein's Universe, BBC, 1979.

Capra, Fritjof. The Tao of Physics, Wildwood House, 1975.

Feinberg, Gerald. What is the World made of? Atoms, leptons, quarks and other tantalising particles, Anchor Press USA, 1977.

Gardner, Martin. The Ambidextrous Universe, Allen Lane, The Penguin Press, 1967.

Ginzburg, Vladimir B. Spiral Grain of the Universe: in search of the Archimedes File, Huntington, 1997; Unified Spiral Field and Matter, Helicola Press, 1999.

Gleiser, Marcelo. The Prophet and the Astronomer: apocalyptic science and the end of the world, Norton, 2004.

Gribbin, John and Plagemann, Stephen. The Jupiter Effect, Macmillan, 1974.

Gribbin, John. White Holes: cosmic gushers in the universe, Paladin, 1977.

Jastrow, Robert. Until the Sun Dies, Souvenir Press, 1978.

Johnston, Alan. The Cosmic Ecosystem: a revised view of cosmology, Wildwood House, 1980.

Keel, John A. The Cosmic Question, Panther, 1978.

Motz, Lloyd. The Universe: its beginning and end, Millington, 1976.

Postle, Denis. Fabric of the Universe, Macmillan, 1976.

Ryan, Peter and Pesek, Ludek. Solar System, Allen Lane, 1978.

Seife, Charles. Alpha and Omega: the search for the beginning and the end of the universe, Doubleday, 2003.

Singh, Simon. Big Bang: the most important scientific discovery of all time and why you need to know about it, Fourth Estate, 2004.

Von Ditfurth, H. Children of the Universe, George Allen & Unwin, 1975.

Warshofsky, Fred. Doomsday: the science of catastrophe, Sphere, 1979.

Weinberg, Steven. The First Three Minutes, Andre Deutsch, 1977.

6: COIL OF LIFE

Bentov, Itzhak. Stalking the Wild Pendulum: on the mechanics of consciousness, Wildwood House, 1978.

Blackmore, Susan. Consciousness: an introduction, Hodder & Stoughton, 2003. Consciousness: a very short introduction, Oxford University Press, 2005.

Dawkins, Richard. The Ancestor's Tale: a pilgrimage to the dawn of life, Weidenfeld & Nicolson, 2004; The Selfish Gene, Oxford University Press, 1976/1989.

Judson, Horace Freeland. The Eighth Day of Creation: the makers of the revolution in biology, Jonathan Cape, 1979; The Search for Solutions, Hutchinson, 1980.

Watson, James D. The Double Helix, Weidenfeld & Nicolson, 1968.

Zohar, Danah. The Quantum Self, Flamingo, 1991.

Zohar, Danah and Marshall, Ian. The Quantum Society: mind, physics and a new social vision, Flamingo, 1994.

7: VORTEX OF TIME

Berlitz, Charles. Doomsday 1999AD, Souvenir Press, 1981.

Bolen, Jean Shinoda. The Tao of Psychology: synchronicity and the self, Wildwood House, 1980.

Drury, Nevill. The New Age: searching for the spiritual self, Thames & Hudson, 2004; Magic and Witchcraft: from shamanism to techno-pagans, Thames & Hudson, 2004.

Humphreys, Christmas. Karma and Rebirth, John Murray, 1943.

Koestler, Arthur. The Roots of Coincidence, Hutchinson, 1972.

Lawton, Ian. Genesis Unveiled: the lost wisdom of our forgotten ancestors, Virgin, 2003.

McGuire, Bill. Surviving Armageddon: solutions for a threatened planet, Oxford University Press, 2005.

Reid, Vera W. Towards Aquarius, Arco USA, 1971.

Seymour, Dr Percy. The Scientific Proof of Astrology: a scientific investigation of how the stars influence human life, Quantum, 2004.

Spangler, David. Revelation: the birth of a new age, Findhorn Foundation, 1971.

Vaughan, Alan. Patterns of Prophecy, Hawthorn USA, 1973; Incredible Coincidence: the baffling world of synchronicity, Corgi, 1981.

Watson, Lyall. Lifetide: a biology of the unconscious, Hodder & Stoughton, 1979.

Wilson, Colin. The Outsider, Phoenix, 2001, orig. Gollancz, 1956; The Occult, Hodder & Stoughton, 1971; Mysteries, Hodder & Stoughton, 1978; From Atlantis to the Sphinx, Virgin, 1997; Alien Dawn: an investigation into the contact experience, Virgin, 1998; Dreaming to Some Purpose: an autobiography, Century, 2004.

Wilson, Colin and Grant, John. Mysteries: a guide to the unknown past, present and future, Chancellor Press, 1994.

Wilson, Colin and Flem-Ath, Rand. The Atlantis Blueprint, Little Brown, 2000.

WEBSITES

Simply entering 'spiral' in Yahoo or Google will produce tens of millions of hits! Here are just a few interesting and useful sites complementary to themes in this book.

Nexus Network Journal: Architecture and Mathematics Online (www.nexusjournal.com) – select 'Search the NNJ', enter 'spiral', and dozens of essays on related topics will appear.

Spirasolaris (www.spirasolaris.ca) – much on the Golden Section and the spiral form in nature, in long historical perspective.

The Geometry Junkyard (www.ics.uci.edu/~eppstein/junkyard/spiral.html) – a fun approach to spirals in profusion.

University of Georgia (www.uga.edu/) – view the seven main types of spiral, as mentioned in Chapter 3: Ritual Art and Nature, by searching for 'Shannon Umberger' on the university homepage. On Shannon's homepage, locate 'Essay #2 – Spirals'.

World Mysteries (www.world-mysteries.com) – select 'Science Mysteries/Fibonacci in Nature'.